RECIPES for

The Nation's Favourite Food

Britain's top 100 dishes

Christine Hall and James Hayes with recipes by Jo' Pratt

BBC

This book is published to accompany the television series entitled
The Nation's Favourite Food, first broadcast on BBC2 in 2003.
Executive producer: Tracy Jeune
Series producer: Richard Bowron
Series director: David DeHaney

Published by BBC Worldwide Limited, Woodlands,
80 Wood Lane, London W12 0TT

First published 2003
Recipes copyright © Jo' Pratt 2003
Text copyright © Christine Hall and James Hayes 2003
The moral right of the authors has been asserted.
Photographs by Jeremy Hudson copyright © BBC Worldwide Limited 2003

ISBN 0 563 48866 2

All recipes serve 4 people unless stated otherwise.
All eggs are size large unless stated otherwise.

Recipes and food preparation for photography: Jo' Pratt
Stylist: Bo Chapman

Commissioning editors: Rachel Copus and Nicky Copeland
Project editor: Sarah Lavelle
Copy editor: Rachel Connolly
Art editor: Sarah Ponder
Production controller: Christopher Tinker
Design: Grade Design Consultants, London

Typeset in DIN
Printed and bound in Italy by LEGO SpA
Colour separations by Radstock Reproductions Ltd, Midsomer Norton

Contents

Foreword by Nigel Slater

'Yes, yes, yes!' I heard myself shouting when I found out that buttered toast was one of the nation's favourite comfort foods in the BBC poll for *The Nation's Favourite Food*. I couldn't agree more. But it was soon followed by a totally mystified 'No!' when I learnt that spaghetti Bolognese – a dish that doesn't even exist in Italy – was Britain's number one dinner. The results got more and more interesting too. An island nation that lists fish and chips as its favourite convenience food is one I am proud to be part of, but what is anyone to make of the fact that pasta salad emerges as one of our favourite outdoor foods. Can anyone like cold pasta that much?

I have to admit there were a few personal disappointments: the fact that oysters weren't higher on the list of Foods of Love; that we seem to prefer carrot cake to chocolate cake or brownies; the inexplicable truth that people still eat chilli con carne when there are so many far more interesting things to eat; and the appearance of sandwiches as our favourite outdoor food (fact: they just curl up in the sun). But there was much good news too: especially that we still love the full English breakfast; our favourite afternoon tea must have not just scones and jam but clotted cream as well; and, joy of joys, Christmas pudding is not far behind the inevitable turkey as our most loved festive food.

Of course, any questionnaire involving food is likely to arouse heated debate, even arguments. It is also likely to involve a few oddball answers. For example, nothing will get me to believe that tapas are among our top party foods, or that steak is something we eat outdoors more than once a year.

One certain fact came out of this poll, which was that we Brits have an appetite for anything that tastes good, regardless of where it comes from. As a nation, we are happy to pinch any culture's best recipes and adopt them into our own everyday diet. We have trawled the world looking for good things to eat and have taken them back to our own kitchens. Just check them out: lamb rogan josh, chicken tikka masala, Thai green curry, risotto, Chinese crispy duck. None of these dishes would have been in the list 20 years ago. They are dishes we have tasted and taken to our hearts almost as dearly as roast beef and Yorkshire pudding. I should like to add that we are also very good at inventing dishes too. You are unlikely to find either sweet-and-sour chicken (our fifth favourite convenience food) or chicken Madras (our eighth) anywhere but in Britain.

One thing seems sure, however. Whilst we are happy to include pain au chocolat in our list of great breakfasts, and welcome chow mein to our list of convenience foods, we still love our traditional dishes. Crumpets, sausage rolls, mince pies and the classic fry-up all get a mention in one list or another. So, thank goodness, do roast pork with crackling, scrambled eggs, steamed pudding, and the great bacon sandwich. Whether you agree or disagree with the nation's choices, one thing is for certain: whatever people may say about British cooking, we certainly know a good thing when we taste it.

Introduction

We have witnessed a food revolution in Britain over the last half century: what we eat and how we eat it has significantly changed. Where once we knew it was Monday because it was cold meat for dinner, or Friday because it was fish, today things are not as simple. Our lifestyles have changed and so have our eating habits. The growth of supermarkets, with more and more choices of food from around the world, has had an impact on what we eat. Having become more affluent as a nation, able to afford more foreign holidays, we have broadened our interest in food from different cultures. Our multi-ethnic society has also contributed greatly to a more informed British palate. Indeed, today, with the increased availability of such cuisines as Chinese, Indian, Italian, Thai, Greek, Mexican, Turkish, Japanese and Australasian, it is now entirely feasible to prepare a meal from a different part of the world every night of the week.

In order to discover the Nation's Favourite Food, we commissioned an online poll. A detailed questionnaire was linked to the BBC Food website asking people a wide range of questions about their eating habits and the foods they would eat if they could choose their all-time favourites. To allow people without access to the Web to take part, a postal questionnaire was also made available. Based on a sample of 2,000 people, from Liskeard to Loch Ness, from Belfast to the Brecon Beacons, we wanted the survey to reflect the favourites of the nation. The results are very much the people's choice – a definitive guide to Great British favourite food, as voted by the Brits.

How, then, do you attempt to chronicle all the favourites? As well as individual tastes, different people like the same food but for different meals. Instead of coming up with just one favourite dish, we combined everyday or weekly mealtimes with special occasions and culinary events to give us themes – breakfast, lunch, dinner, food of love, take-away or convenience food, outdoor food, comfort food, afternoon tea, party food and festive food. Everyone was asked to vote for their favourite food in each category. We also asked for some personal details so that we could examine whether there were differences between men and women, between the young and not so young and between the regions and 'nations' that make up Britain. In this way we were able to see, for instance, that roast chicken was four times more popular for lunch in Northern Ireland (where 54 per cent voted it their favourite lunch dish) than it was in Wales, and that those aged 35 or under are much more likely to turn to chocolate for comfort than those over 35.

But what you eat during the week is not always the same as what you have at the weekend. Many said that you make do with just a coffee or tea and toast for breakfast during the week, but like to celebrate the beginning of the weekend and indulge in the 'full Monty' fry-up when you have the time to do so. The traditional Sunday lunch is still revered by many people up and down the country. For many of you, this is still a special family time, the one meal of the week when all the family members sit down and reintroduce themselves after a hectic and fragmented week. But not everyone agreed, and many more of you now insist that Sunday is the one day when you can't be bothered to cook, so you rely on a pub lunch with friends instead.

We called on the services of several well-known cooks to give us their opinions of what finally appeared in the lists of top ten dishes, and we asked them for their personal anecdotes of growing up in the world of food. Gary Rhodes talked to us about his experiences of a family Christmas, Gordon Ramsay enthused about dinner, love and parties; Nigel Slater admitted a few surprising personal dislikes; Madhur Jaffrey gave us an insight to the introduction of Indian food to Britain; Ainsley Harriott revealed what food he'd choose to woo his wife; and Rick Stein was thrilled to discover the nation had included fish more than once in their final votes.

It has been said that in recent years we have become obsessed with food in Britain. Certainly there has been much debate about how British food is changing and whether we have lost our traditional dishes in an ever-changing sea of outside influences. What we have found in *The Nation's Favourite Food* is that while some of our favourites celebrate and reflect our multicultural society, we are also still very much holding on to our more traditional dishes. What follows is a definitive guide to Great British eating habits and a wonderful collection of the nation's top 100 dishes.

1:
Nation's Favourite Breakfast

Three cheers for the full English breakfast! Despite the fact that we've become more health-conscious, the great British fry-up still rules the roost as the nation's number one breakfast. We usually indulge in a full English breakfast when we need a little comfort, but whether it's a weekend treat or an occasional blow-out, the combination of bacon, eggs, sausage, fried bread, black pudding, mushrooms and tomatoes still satisfies our British taste buds.

It's said that breakfast is the most important meal of the day and yet, according to our survey, four per cent of us skip it altogether, without even a cup of tea or coffee to kick-start the day. Busy lifestyles or a lack of hunger in the morning are the usual reasons given, and with the popularity of coffee-shop culture spreading throughout the country, it's just as easy to pick up breakfast on the move. Unlike any other meal, our breakfast is based on habit: most of us eat exactly the same thing every morning but would soon tire if we ate the same thing for dinner every day.

One of the most surprising statistics to come out of our survey is that only seven per cent of people in Scotland voted for porridge as their favourite breakfast. Surely it's not a cliché to say that porridge is a Scottish national dish? Although porridge may be out of favour for some, as a nation we still consume 47 million gallons every year. The World Porridge-making Champion, Duncan Hilditch,

Duncan Hilditch's Porridge   Serves 2

- 1 cup of medium
  oatmeal
- 4 cups of water
- ³/₄ teaspoon salt
- large pinch of sugar
- 1 cup of double cream
soft brown sugar

1. Put the oatmeal and the water into a saucepan over a medium heat. Once it has come to the boil, turn down the heat and simmer for 4¹/₂ minutes, stirring constantly with a wooden spoon.

2. Add the salt and a large pinch of sugar, and just before serving stir in most of the cream, giving the porridge a final beat. Sprinkle with soft brown sugar to taste and an extra drizzle of cream.

believes his success lies in his spurtle, the carved wooden stick he uses to stir the porridge. He whittled this himself from Scottish oak salvaged from a giant vat that held maturing whisky for 250 years, and keeps it permanently soaked in malt whisky. He makes his porridge in the traditional way with water and salt and insists it should be stirred in a clockwise direction to ward off the devil.

Some of the dishes that failed to reach the top ten are notable by their absence. The mainstay of childhood breakfasts and Queen Victoria's favourite, the humble boiled egg, came in at a disappointing number twelve. Award-winning cookery writer Nigel Slater has revealed a surprising aversion to boiled and poached eggs, having been force-fed them as a child: 'There's something so disgusting about the smell of a boiled egg when you cut off the top. I used to wake up on a Sunday morning and I could smell them cooking. I would come downstairs and my father would shovel eggs into my mouth to make me into a big, strong lad like my brother. It was the most horrendous experience of my life. Now I can't even look at them.'

Fish dishes seem to have lost their appeal as well, although kippers and kedgeree may be making a welcome comeback thanks to some top hotels and restaurateurs who are now including them on their breakfast menus.

Even though we don't always eat breakfast, it still forms part of our understanding of what it is to be British. And now that it's possible to get a full fried breakfast 24 hours a day, seven days a week, it's turned into a dish that could easily sustain us for lunch, dinner or even a midnight feast.

1

Full English Breakfast

A quarter of the nation voted this their number one breakfast, with twice as many men enjoying a full fry-up as women, especially those in the North West of England. This version is cooked using a flat grill plate, but a large, heavy-based frying pan is a good alternative.

Stress-free Full English Breakfast

Per person, allow:
- 2 sausages
- 2–3 rashers of bacon
- 2 flat mushrooms
- 1–2 ripe tomatoes
- 1 thick slice of black pudding
- 1 large egg
- 1 slice of bread

Heat the flat grill plate over a low heat, on top of 2 rings/flames if it fits, and brush sparingly with light olive oil.

SAUSAGES

Always buy sausages with a high meat content. Cook these first. Add the sausages to the hot grill plate (the coolest part if there is one) and allow to cook slowly for about 15–20 minutes, turning occasionally, until golden. After the first 10 minutes, increase the heat to medium before beginning to cook the other ingredients. If you are struggling for space, completely cook the sausages and keep hot on a plate in the oven.

BACON

Choose between back or streaky, smoked or unsmoked bacon; generally, dry-cure has the best flavour. Snip a few small cuts into the fatty edge of the bacon. Place the bacon straight on to the grill plate and fry for 2–4 minutes each side or until your preferred crispiness is reached. Like the sausages, the cooked bacon can be kept hot on a plate in the oven.

MUSHROOMS

Brush away any dirt using a pastry brush and trim the stalk level with the mushroom top. Season with salt and pepper and drizzle over a little olive oil. Place stalk-side up on the grill plate and cook for 1–2 minutes before turning and cooking for a further 3–4 minutes. Avoid moving the mushrooms too much while cooking, as this releases the natural juices, making them soggy.

TOMATOES

Cut the tomatoes across the centre (or in half lengthways if using plum tomatoes), and with a small, sharp knife remove the green 'eye'. Season with salt and pepper and drizzle with a little olive oil. Place cut-side down on the grill plate and cook without moving for 2 minutes. Gently turn over and season again. Cook for a further 2–3 minutes until tender but still holding their shape.

BLACK PUDDING

Cut the black pudding into 3–4 slices and remove the skin. Place on the grill plate and cook for $1\frac{1}{2}$–2 minutes each side until slightly crispy.

FRIED BREAD

For 'proper' fried bread it's best to cook it in a separate pan. Ideally, use bread that is a couple of days old. Heat a frying pan to a medium heat and cover the base with oil. Add the bread and cook for 2–3 minutes each side until crispy and golden. If the pan becomes too dry, add a little more oil. For a richer flavour, add a knob of butter after you turn the slice.

FRIED EGGS

Break the egg straight into the pan with the fried bread and leave for 30 seconds. Add a good knob of butter and lightly splash/baste the egg with the butter when melted. Cook to your preferred stage, season and gently remove with a fish slice.

Once all the ingredients are cooked, serve on warm plates and enjoy straight away with a good squeeze of tomato ketchup or brown sauce.

2   Cereal

With nearly a quarter of the population voting for cereal, it's clear that it is still an important part of our diet. By the early 1900s, the breakfast cereal market was booming, with manufacturers claiming their cereals could cure all ills. Whichever cereal you prefer, try making your own cereal mix for a change. First, you need to make your own basic toasted muesli. This will keep fresh in an airtight container for several weeks.

Basic Muesli

- 200 g (7 oz) jumbo porridge oats
- 25 g (1 oz) flaked bran or wheatgerm
- 75 g (3 oz) barley or rye flakes
- 50 g (2 oz) hazelnuts, lightly crushed
- 50 g (2 oz) flaked almonds
- 50 g (2 oz) sultanas
- 50 g (2 oz) dried, ready-to-eat apricots, roughly chopped
- 50 g (2 oz) dried, ready-to-eat figs, roughly chopped

1. Pre-heat the oven to 160°C/325°F/Gas Mark 3.

2. Place the oats, flaked bran or wheatgerm, barley or rye flakes, hazelnuts and almonds on a large baking tray and toast in the oven for 10 minutes, shaking and turning in the tray halfway through. Take the tray from the oven and leave to cool: this should take only about 10 minutes.

3. Mix the toasted ingredients with the sultanas, apricots and figs. These fruits are only suggestions: you can use whatever you prefer, for example dried apple, mango, papaya, dates or cherries.

You can eat this muesli straight away with milk or, for a special occasion, create the impressive-looking breakfast treat described below:

Feeling Fruity Muesli Layer   Serves 1

- a large handful of blueberries, raspberries or strawberries, chopped
- 2 handfuls of basic muesli (see above)
- ½ apple, grated
- squeeze of lemon juice
- apple juice or milk
- Greek yoghurt and honey, to serve

1. Place half the soft fruit in the bottom of a tall drinking glass or dish.

2. In a bowl, mix together the muesli, grated apple and lemon juice. Spoon half this mixture on top of the fresh fruits and repeat with another layer of fruit, then muesli. Pour over enough apple juice or milk to cover.

3. This can now be left in the fridge for a few hours or overnight. Just before serving, top with a layer of Greek yoghurt and a spoonful of honey.

3   Toast

A fifth of the nation have toast for breakfast and almost a third of all Scots start the day with toast. Thick-cut processed white bread popped into the toaster straight from the packet makes perfect toast in some people's eyes, especially if it's thickly buttered while still hot. Others prefer a rough, hand-cut slice of day-old crumbly granary under the grill.

You can make toast however you like, but here's a suggestion of what to put on it to add a bit of sugar and spice to your morning.

Sweet Cinnamon Buttered Toast

- 1½ tablespoons caster sugar, plus extra to taste
- ½ teaspoon ground cinnamon, plus extra to taste
- 50 g (2 oz) unsalted butter, softened
- grated orange zest (optional)

1. Mix the caster sugar and ground cinnamon into the butter, adding extra sugar or cinnamon until you reach the right sweetness and spiciness for your taste. If you fancy an additional fruity flavour, add a touch of grated orange zest.

2. Toast your bread under the grill on one side, then remove and spread a generous helping of the cinnamon butter over the untoasted side. Place back under the grill, butter-side up, and toast until the butter is bubbling and the edges of the bread are golden. The butter can easily be made in large quantities and kept in the fridge or freezer so you have plenty on hand for when you fancy it (although it won't last long as it's very moreish).

4   Coffee

Latte, cappuccino, Americano, espresso, filter and instant – just a small selection of the types of coffee available today. Fourteen per cent of the nation enjoys coffee for breakfast, and the over-55s are particularly keen on a caffeine kick-start to the day. You don't need an expensive machine to make a cappuccino at home – you can get authentic results with a stove-top espresso maker and a milk frother.

The Perfect Home Cappuccino   Makes 2 cups

- ½ coffee cup of water
- 2–3 level tablespoons freshly ground coffee
- 1½ coffee cups of skimmed milk
- chocolate powder, to garnish

1. Pour the water into the base of the stove-top espresso maker. Then pack the freshly ground coffee into the filter using the back of a spoon. The amount you use really depends on the strength of the coffee beans. Screw on the top and place on the hob over a medium heat.

2. While the espresso is brewing, heat the milk to just below boiling point. Skimmed milk is the best to use as it holds its froth for longer because of the lower fat content. Once the milk is hot, whisk with a battery-operated milk frother. If you don't have one, place the milk in a large cafetière and pump the plunger 10–15 times until you have plenty of froth – approximately half froth and half milk.

3. Pour the espresso into warm cups, then, using a large spoon to hold back the froth, pour the milk into the cups. Top with the froth, leaving a visible brown rim around the edge for an authentic look. Sprinkle with the chocolate.

The best cappuccino should be one third espresso, one third milk and one third froth. You'll find the more often you make them, the better they'll become.

5 Fresh or Stewed Fruit

Women favour fruit for breakfast, especially in the South West of England. Sure to awaken the morning taste buds, this grapefruit dish is based on a classic recipe with a modern twist.

Grilled Ginger Grapefruit Serves 2–4

- 2 grapefruit, preferably pink
- 2 pieces of stem ginger in syrup
- Greek yoghurt, to serve

1. Pre-heat the grill to a medium heat.

2. Cut the grapefruit in half and remove any large seeds. To make it easier to eat, loosen each section with a serrated knife by cutting along the membranes and around the pith. Now place cut-side up on a baking sheet.

3. Chop the ginger into small dice and scatter over the grapefruit halves. Drizzle about 2 teaspoons of the ginger syrup over each and place under the grill for about 5 minutes or until it begins to turn golden.

4. Eat the grapefruit straight away with a dollop of Greek yoghurt on top.

TIPS

If you want an even fruitier flavour, scoop the flesh and seeds from 1–2 passion fruit over each grapefruit half after grilling.

If you want to save time in the morning, put the ginger grapefruit in the fridge overnight before grilling. Marinating like this gives the flavours a chance to develop, so that the grapefruit tastes even better when grilled.

6 Bacon Sandwich

According to our survey, if you're under 25 you're three times more likely to enjoy a bacon butty for breakfast than your over-55-year-old parents. The bacon sarnie is a great source of controversy. Back bacon or streaky? White or brown bread? Ketchup or brown sauce? The combinations are endless, but regardless of your preference, this is how to make it.

The Best Bacon Sarnie Makes 2

- 6–8 rashers of rindless smoked or unsmoked back or streaky bacon (thick-cut for a meatier sarnie)
- light olive oil
- 4 thick slices of fresh cut bread (the fresher the better)
- tomato ketchup or brown sauce (your choice)

1. To get a really crisp edge, snip a few small cuts in the fat around each bacon rasher. This will also stop it from curling up too much when cooking. It's best to buy dry-cure bacon if you can, as less water is released when frying, ensuring really crisp fat (the best bit) and a better flavour.

2. Place a large frying pan over a medium heat and add a trickle of oil.

3. Lay the bacon in the pan and cook for about 3–4 minutes on each side or until it's as crispy as you prefer. Remove the bacon and divide between 2 slices of bread. Spread either tomato ketchup or brown sauce on to the remaining 2 slices and place sauce-side down in the pan. Leave for about a minute to absorb all the juices in the pan, also warming (but not toasting) the bread. The other 2 pieces will be warmed through by the hot bacon on top, with any bacon fat seeping through the bread. Assemble the sandwiches and eat straight away.

7 Scrambled Egg on Toast

We've all had rubbery scrambled egg on soggy toast in B&Bs and hotels around the country and wondered how they could get it so wrong. Good scrambled egg is hard to beat, and easy to make if you follow the rules. Michelin-starred chef Gordon Ramsay recommends adding cream or full-fat milk at the end of cooking to give the eggs a creamy texture and to stop them cooking further. This version works on the same principle.

Creamy Scrambled Egg on Herby Buttered Muffins Serves 2

- 3 tablespoons salted butter, at room temperature
- a handful of mixed fresh herbs, such as parsley, chives, tarragon or basil, chopped
- 2 white English muffins
- 4 large eggs
- 4 tablespoons single cream
- celery salt
- freshly ground black pepper

1. In a bowl, mix together 2 tablespoons of the butter with the chopped herbs.

2. Split the muffins in half and toast until golden brown. While the muffins are toasting, place the remaining butter in a non-stick saucepan and melt over a gentle heat.

3. Break the eggs into a large jug, add the cream, season with a pinch of celery salt and pepper and whisk lightly. Swirl the melted butter in the pan then pour in the eggs. Leave for a few seconds without stirring, then stir fairly briskly using a wooden fork, making sure you get into the edges of the pan. Once the eggs are softly set but before they are fully cooked, remove from the heat as they'll continue cooking in the pan. This will give you a really creamy finish, rather than something that resembles rubber!

4. Spread the herb butter over the hot toasted muffins, and place the bottom halves on 2 plates. Spoon the scrambled egg on top, add a little freshly ground black pepper, and finish with the other muffin halves. Serve straight away.

As an alternative you could try making different-flavoured butters:
- tomato ketchup and chive
- garlic salt and parsley
- chopped fresh or dried flaked red chilli
- anchovy, lemon juice and parsley
- mild curry powder
- pesto

Or try adding flavours to the scrambled egg:
- crispy fried bacon pieces
- strips of smoked salmon and crème fraîche rather than the cream
- chopped fresh herbs
- mild curry powder
- fresh coriander and chopped chilli

8

Croissant or Pain au Chocolat

The croissant was first introduced to this country by Pillsbury Dough and was available from the cold counter at supermarkets. Remember the roll of pastry you unfolded and popped in the oven to form a perfect crescent shape? Many would argue it tasted nothing like the real thing, but for some it was their first introduction to the Continental breakfast.

Now, with coffee shops popping up all over Britain, many of us grab a coffee and a croissant on our way to work rather than prepare breakfast at home. But if you buy plain croissants from the supermarket you can make your own fresh version of pain au chocolat for a weekend treat.

Melting Chocolate and Almond Croissant

- 4 croissants
- 200 g (7 oz) good-quality plain or milk chocolate
- a handful of toasted flaked almonds
- icing sugar and/or cocoa powder, for dusting

1. Pre-heat the oven to 180°C/350°F/Gas Mark 4.

2. Slice each croissant in half and set the 4 bases on a baking sheet. Break the chocolate into small pieces and scatter on top, then sprinkle over some almonds. Sit the other croissant halves on top and put in the oven. Cook for 5–6 minutes, or until the croissants are warm and crispy on the outside and the chocolate is just beginning to ooze through the edges. For a fancy finish, dust with some icing sugar or cocoa powder and eat straight away.

TIP

If you don't have a sweet tooth or you're in the mood for a savoury filling, place some grated cheese (Gruyère is delicious) and a slice of ham into a halved croissant, and cook for the same amount of time. Spice it up with a touch of mustard spread inside the croissant before baking.

9   Porridge

10   Yoghurt

Until the 1950s, universities in Scotland had a day off in January to mark Mealy Monday. This was a chance for students to follow the tradition of 18th-century crofters and farmers, who made large amounts of porridge for their porridge 'drawers'. It was then left to go cold before being sliced and taken to work each day to sustain them through long hours of manual work. Porridge is still a great source of energy at the start of the day. Choose between pinhead, rolled or whole oats, and you can add Drambuie, cream, golden syrup or a sprinkling of brown sugar. If you find the Scots way with porridge too frugal, try this full-flavour, full-fat version.

Podgy Porridge   Serves 4–6

- 900 ml (1$\frac{1}{2}$ pints) full-fat milk
- 225 g (8 oz) porridge oats
- 1 tablespoon caster sugar
- $\frac{1}{2}$ teaspoon ground cinnamon
- pinch of salt
- 200 ml (7 fl oz) single cream or milk
- golden syrup or brown sugar, to serve

1. Place the full-fat milk in a large, non-stick saucepan and bring to the boil. Briskly stir in the oats, sugar, cinnamon and salt. Bring to a very gentle simmer and cook for 8 minutes, stirring occasionally. Once the mixture is cooked, add the cream or milk and stir until heated but not boiling. You will now have lovely, rich, creamy porridge.

2. Spoon into warm bowls and, for ultimate extravagance, drizzle with lots of sticky golden syrup or sprinkle with brown sugar.

TIP

If guilt takes over and you don't want to go the whole hog, try a less podgy version of the porridge using semi-skimmed or skimmed milk. You can add extra milk in place of the cream at the end of the cooking time.

Supermarket shelves heave with hundreds of varieties of yoghurt, confirming the fact that in the last ten years our consumption at breakfast time has increased by nearly 50 per cent. In our survey, yoghurt is three times more popular in the Midlands and East of England than in Wales and the North East.

This yoghurt smoothie is guaranteed to kick-start everyone into action.

Red Rooster Smoothie   Serves 2–3

- 2 x 125 ml (4$\frac{1}{4}$ fl oz) fruit-flavoured yoghurt, ideally strawberry, raspberry or cherry
- 400 g (14 oz) fresh or frozen summer berries
- 300 ml ($\frac{1}{2}$ pint) cranberry juice
- 2 bananas, peeled and roughly chopped

Place all of the ingredients in a liquidizer and blitz until smooth. Pour into tall glasses and enjoy straight away. If you want your smoothie on the move, pour it into a clean 'take-away' coffee cup with a lid and drink it through a straw. If you're fussy about pips or seeds or you're worried they'll get stuck in your teeth, strain the smoothie through a sieve before pouring into glasses.

WARNING: Frozen berries are very loud when being blitzed and are guaranteed to wake up the entire household as well as yourself.

2: Nation's Favourite Lunch

Tradition still rules when it comes to the British lunch. Yes, the stalwart of Sunday lunchtimes around the country – from Liskeard to Loch Ness; from Belfast to the Brecon Beacons – is roast beef and Yorkshire pudding, voted the nation's number one lunch by a third of the voting population.

But lunch as a meal has completely changed over the years. Until 30 or 40 years ago, lunch was a regular feature in any family household and children would often come home from school during the week to enjoy a proper cooked meal with their parents. It was the time of day to consume the biggest meal, leaving 'tea' to be taken after a hard day's work or a busy school schedule. Now, unless you're a businessman or lady of leisure who chooses to 'do' lunch, the break in the middle of the day has diminished to a quick light snack or a pre-packed meal. Consequently, the sandwich has come into its own. And it's not just the humble cheese and tomato or egg and cress sandwich; we're talking about a complete meal between two slices of bread. The combinations are endless – roast chicken with stuffing and cranberry

sauce; mozzarella, tomato, avocado and mayonnaise; smoked ham with cheese, lettuce and mustard dressing; chicken tikka with mango chutney; a whole English breakfast in a roll. And then there's the bread – not just brown or white, but baguette, ciabatta, wholemeal, granary, focaccia, soda, sourdough or rye. The sandwich trade is booming and looks set to continue that way.

Because we eat lunch so frugally during the week, when the weekend arrives it seems we're much more likely to indulge in a leisurely meal. Whether it's a casual Saturday lunch with friends or a colossal feast with all the family on a Sunday, there's something about lunch at the weekend that suggests indulgence. Nigel Slater looks forward to a Sunday roast, but with reservations: 'Sunday lunch is a performance. It's a meal that I love but I don't like the way we do it. I like the crackling, I like the horseradish sauce, the apple sauce, the mustard, the roast potatoes – especially the one that sticks to the side of the roasting tin. I love the Yorkshire pudding and the gravy, I adore it, I absolutely love it, but not all on the same plate. When it comes piled up high it's more like a dog's dinner.'

The tradition of Sunday lunch is part of the British psyche and roast beef will always be a favourite. Yorkshire pudding was originally designed to be eaten as a separate course served up before the meat with ladles of hot gravy. It was a cheap and easy way to fill you up so you wouldn't need as much expensive meat on your plate. The batter pudding was traditionally made in a large roasting tin and cut into squares for serving. In some households any leftovers were spread with jam for a filling dessert. But if you're not in the mood for cooking your own roast lunch, you can get a decent pub roast for under a tenner. Some of the top French restaurants in the country even serve up traditional roast beef, pork or lamb at the weekends, recognizing the fact that we crave our national dishes just as much as the French, Italian, Asian and Australasian foods that have become a part of our diet in recent years.

1

Roast Beef and Yorkshire Pudding

This classic Sunday dish is most popular with the over-55s but it still appeals to the younger generation. Nearly 36 per cent of under-25s voted it their favourite, proving we're still traditionalists at heart and roast beef and Yorkshire pud are here to stay.

This recipe is for beef off the bone, which makes it much easier to carve, but if you're particularly adept with the carving knife a rib of beef on the bone will give you the most authentic and succulent roast. For perfect Yorkshires it's best to make the batter in advance (at least 30 minutes; preferably overnight if you can), and the addition of an extra egg white gives the batter a lift and the puddings a light and fluffy finish.

If you have any leftover puddings, you can make a simple dessert: warm some golden syrup, pour it into the hollow of the individual pudding and serve it with some chilled pouring cream. Scrumptious.

Roast Rib of Beef with Mustard and Thyme Yorkshire Puddings and Red Wine Gravy   Serves 6

- vegetable or groundnut oil
- flaked sea salt and freshly ground black pepper
- approx. 2.25 kg (5 lb) boned and rolled rib joint of beef
- 6 shallots, peeled and left whole
- 2 carrots, peeled and cut in half
- 1 bulb of garlic, cut in half across the centre
- few sprigs of fresh thyme

1. Pre-heat the oven to 190°C/375°F/Gas Mark 5.

2. Heat a good glug of oil in a large roasting tray on the hob. Rub plenty of salt and pepper over the beef and colour it in the hot oil on all sides for a few minutes. Remove the beef from the tray and add the shallots, carrots, garlic and thyme to the tray, then sit the beef on top. Cook in the oven for about 1¾ hours for medium rare; add another 15 minutes for medium, and 30 minutes for medium–well done. During the cooking time, baste the beef every so often with any juices in the pan. If the bottom of the pan seems a little dry, add a little of the stock or water measured for the gravy (see overleaf). Once it is cooked, transfer the beef on to a plate and loosely cover with foil. Retain the contents of the roasting tray for the gravy. The beef can now be left to rest in a warm place for 20–25 minutes, giving you just the right amount of time to cook the Yorkshire puddings and gravy.

(CONTINUED OVERLEAF)

1 continued

Mustard and Thyme Yorkshire Puddings   Makes 12

- 225 g (8 oz) plain flour
- pinch of salt
- 2 teaspoons English mustard powder
- 3 eggs, beaten
- 1 egg white
- 1 teaspoon fresh thyme leaves, or $1/2$ teaspoon dried thyme
- 300–400 ml (10–14 fl oz) milk
- vegetable or groundnut oil, for cooking

1. Pre-heat the oven to 220°C/425°F/Gas Mark 7 and place 1–2 deep muffin tins in to pre-heat.

2. Sift the flour, salt and mustard powder into a large bowl and whisk in the beaten eggs, egg white, thyme and enough milk to give a smooth, thick batter about the consistency of double cream. The batter is best left for at least 30 minutes, or if you can make it the day before and keep it in the fridge, that's even better. This will give you really smooth, well-risen Yorkshires. Rewhisk the batter just before using, adding any extra milk to return to the double-cream consistency. Pour into a jug. If you're making the mixture on the day, you can do this while the beef is cooking.

3. Remove the muffin tins from the oven and pour a good drop of oil into each hole. Return to the oven for a few minutes until the oil is almost smoking. Carefully take out of the oven and pour the batter into the tins, almost filling each hole. Return to the oven and cook for 25–30 minutes, or until golden and crispy. While the Yorkshires are cooking, filling the kitchen with the wonderful aroma of thyme, you can make the gravy.

Red Wine Gravy

- 1 heaped tablespoon plain flour
- $1/2$ bottle full-bodied red wine
- 450 ml ($3/4$ pint) beef stock or water

1. Pour away any excess oil from the roasting tray and place it with all the sticky vegetables back on the hob over a high heat. Vigorously stir in the flour and then pour in the red wine and beef stock or water. Bring to the boil, cooking for about 8 minutes until slightly thickened. Pour in any juices from the resting beef, then season with salt and pepper.

2. Strain through a sieve, pushing through all the juices from the vegetables, and serve in a warm jug with thick slices of the rested roast beef and the perfectly risen Yorkshire puds.

2 Sandwich

Sandwiches are the favoured weekday lunch of 29 per cent of the population, but in Northern Ireland nearly half voted for a sandwich lunch. Young people especially enjoy this snack, probably because it's easy to eat and goes so well with a can of something fizzy and a bag of crisps. There's always somewhere to buy a sandwich for lunch, but it's far cheaper, fresher and healthier to make your own (see also pages 86 and 126).

Cheddar and Chunky Beetroot Mayonnaise Baguette   Serves 2

- 100 g (4 oz) cooked beetroot, preferably not in vinegar
- 2 tablespoons mayonnaise
- 4 spring onions
- 1 fresh medium baguette
- 1 small bag of rocket leaves or watercress

- 150 g (5 oz) creamy mature Cheddar cheese, coarsely grated
- flaked sea salt and freshly ground black pepper

1. Place half of the beetroot in a small food processor or blender with the mayonnaise and blitz until smooth and a vibrant pink colour. Chop the spring onions and remaining beetroot as big or small as you want and stir into the mayonnaise.

2. Split the baguette in half and fill with the rocket or watercress, Cheddar and beetroot mayonnaise. Season with salt and pepper before cutting in two and eating.

BLT Club Sarnie   Makes 2

- 8 rashers of rindless smoked or unsmoked streaky bacon (dry-cure if possible)
- trickle of olive oil
- 6 slices of white or granary bread
- good-quality mayonnaise, for spreading
- 2 ripe tomatoes, sliced
- 2 Little Gem lettuces
- flaked sea salt and freshly ground black pepper
- ¹/₂ small red onion, sliced
- 1 small ripe avocado, peeled, stoned and sliced

8 cocktail sticks or alternative

1. Snip a few small cuts in the fat around each bacon rasher. Fry in the olive oil over a medium heat for about 3–4 minutes each side until golden and crispy.

2. While the bacon is cooking, toast the bread and spread 2 slices thickly with mayonnaise. Layer the tomatoes and lettuce leaves on top and season well. Spread mayonnaise on to 2 more pieces of toast and sit these on top. Divide the cooked bacon, onion and avocado between the two, season well and finish with the remaining toast, pressing down lightly.

3. Cut into quarters (a serrated bread knife is perfect) and secure each one with a cocktail stick for that classic bistro finish. Eat this straight away to enjoy it at its best – hot crispy bacon with oozing mayonnaise.

TIPS

Add some crushed garlic, lemon juice, Tabasco sauce, chopped herbs, freshly grated Parmesan cheese or mustard to the mayonnaise for additional flavour. Cooked chicken tastes great with the bacon, or on its own instead of the bacon.

3

Roast Lamb with Mint Sauce

Those in the South West of England consume more roast lamb than any-where else in the country; not surprising, as there are around 5 million sheep grazing the hills and fields of Devon, Cornwall and Somerset.

Shoulder of lamb is often tastier than leg as there's more fat running through the meat, guaranteeing its succulence and soft texture. This stuffed boned shoulder looks impressive and the flavour is exquisite. Ask the butcher to remove the bone if you don't feel confident doing it yourself.

Roast Shoulder of Lamb with Apricot, Cranberry and Rosemary Stuffing and Gravy   Serves 6

- 1.75 kg (4 lb) shoulder of lamb, boned
- 2 long stalks of rosemary (optional)
- olive oil
- salt and freshly ground black pepper

STUFFING
- 100 g (4 oz) fresh white breadcrumbs
- 2 tablespoons chopped fresh rosemary
- 10 dried, ready-to-eat apricots, quartered
- 100 g (4 oz) dried cranberries
- 8 spring onions, finely chopped
- 1 egg, beaten

GRAVY
- 700 ml (1½ pints) lamb stock or water
- 2 large glasses white wine
- 2 tablespoons cranberry sauce
- 1 heaped tablespoon cornflour, mixed with 1 tablespoon water

1. Pre-heat the oven to 200°C/400°F/Gas Mark 6.

2. Mix together all of the stuffing ingredients and season well with salt and pepper.

3. Lay the lamb on a board, boned-side up, and spread over the stuffing. Roll up and tie in three or four places with string to hold in shape while cooking. For additional flavour and to secure the meat, skewer a couple of rosemary stalks through as well if you wish.

4. Place in a roasting tray, rub some oil over the lamb and tray, then season well with salt and pepper. Pour 150 ml (¼ pint) of the lamb stock or water for the gravy into the base of the tray. Cook in the oven for 20 minutes before reducing the temperature to 180°C/350°F/Gas Mark 4 and cooking for a further 1 hour 20 minutes, basting occasionally with any juices. Once the meat is cooked, remove it from the tray and sit it on a plate in a warm place to rest.

5. To make the gravy, drain any excess fat from the tray and put the tray over a medium heat. Pour in the remaining lamb stock, the white wine and cranberry sauce and boil for 3–4 minutes. Stir in the cornflour and cook until thickened. If you prefer a thicker gravy, add a further tablespoon of cornflour. Season with salt and pepper and pour into a jug.

Serve with Mint Sauce (see page 152) and vegetables of your choice.

4

Roast Chicken

A roast chicken has to be one of the easiest meals to prepare. In Northern Ireland over half the population voted it their favourite Sunday lunch, which is double the national average. There are many ingredients that marry perfectly with the flavours of chicken – herbs such as tarragon, thyme, sage or rosemary stuffed inside, butter pushed under the skin, halved lemons, shallots and garlic roasted around the chicken – or simply season and butter the bird and baste it frequently during the cooking. It's worth paying a bit more for a free-range chicken to guarantee you get the most flavoursome of birds. The stuffing muffins served with this dish (see overleaf) really make it stand out, and they particularly appeal to kids.

Herby Lemon Roast Chicken with Stuffing Muffins

- 6 sticks of celery
- 4 small onions, halved
- 1 bulb of garlic, cut in half across the centre
- 1 large lemon
- 2 glasses of dry sherry (about 200 ml/7 fl oz in total)
- 2 kg (4½ lb) chicken, preferably free-range
- 4 bay leaves
- 3–4 sprigs each of sage, rosemary, oregano and thyme
- olive oil
- flaked sea salt and freshly ground black pepper
- 250 ml (8 fl oz) chicken stock
- 1 tablespoon honey
- 2 tablespoons double cream

1. Pre-heat the oven to 200°C/400°F/Gas Mark 6.

2. Place the celery, onion, and one half of the garlic bulb in a roasting tray. Peel the zest of the lemon with a vegetable peeler and scatter on top, keeping a couple of strips aside.

3. Pour a glass of sherry and a sherry glass of water over the vegetables and sit the chicken on top. Halve the zested lemon and squeeze the juice over the chicken. Stuff the squeezed halves inside the chicken with 3 of the bay leaves and the remaining garlic.

4. Loosely tie the herb sprigs, the remaining bay leaf and reserved lemon zest strips with a piece of string and lay on top of the chicken. If you have any extra herbs, stuff a few sprigs into the chicken for added flavour. Pour a generous glug of olive oil over the chicken and herbs, then season with salt and pepper. Place in the oven for 1¼ hours, basting a couple of times during cooking with any juices. At the end of cooking the chicken should have beautiful golden skin with lots of juices in the base of the tray. Check it is cooked by cutting through the leg; the juices should run clear. If not, place back in the oven for 10 minutes.

(CONTINUED OVERLEAF)

4 continued

5. Pour the juices out of the chicken cavity into the tray and sit the chicken on a plate in a warm place covered with foil. Place the tray over a high heat and stir in the chicken stock, the remaining sherry (if you haven't drunk it by now) and the honey. Scrape all the sticky bits from the base and bring to the boil. Cook for a few minutes before stirring in the cream and seasoning with salt and pepper. Strain the gravy into a jug and serve with the chicken and the stuffing muffins.

Bacon and Sweetcorn 'Stuffing' Muffins   Makes 8

- 200 g (7 oz) unsmoked pancetta or bacon, diced
- 1 large onion, chopped
- 1 clove of garlic, crushed
- 225 g (8 oz) fresh breadcrumbs
- 150 g (5 oz) cooked sweetcorn
- 6 halves of sun-dried tomato, chopped
- a small handful of flat-leaf parsley, chopped
- 1 teaspoon chopped fresh oregano or thyme
- 2 eggs, beaten
- flaked sea salt and freshly ground black pepper
- small knob of butter

1. Fry the pancetta or bacon in a dry frying pan for 3–4 minutes until crisp and golden. Remove from the pan with a slotted spoon and leave to cool. To make full use of the bacon flavour, fry the onion and garlic in the fat left in the pan until softened. If the bacon fat is too dark to use, just wipe out the pan and cook the onion and garlic in a little olive oil. Leave to cool with the pancetta or bacon.

2. Once they are cool, mix together with the breadcrumbs, sweetcorn, sun-dried tomato, parsley, oregano or thyme and beaten eggs. Season with salt and pepper, then mix well. Spoon into 8 muffin papers in a muffin tin. Dot a little butter on top of each one and then bake for 25 minutes in the oven with the chicken until just golden. Remove from the oven and serve straight away with the herby roast chicken and gravy.

=5

Roast Pork
with Crackling and Apple Sauce

We consume 13.3 kg (about 29 lb) of pork per person per year and, according to our survey, the older generation enjoys a roast pork lunch more than anyone else.

One of the best things about roast pork is the crackling, as long as it's really crispy. The best way to guarantee a crunch factor is to buy your pork a couple of days before cooking and leave on a plate uncovered in the fridge, which gives the skin a chance to dry out completely.

Roast Loin of Pork with Crispy Crackling and Cider Gravy   Serves 6

- 2 kg (4½ lb) loin of pork, boned and rolled, with skin attached, and scored several times
- vegetable oil
- flaked sea salt and freshly ground black pepper
- 3 large onions
- 1 tablespoon plain flour
- 1–2 teaspoons coarse grain mustard
- 250 ml (8 fl oz) cider
- 250 ml (8 fl oz) vegetable stock
- 50–75 ml (2–3 fl oz) double cream (optional)

1. Pre-heat the oven to 200°C/400°F/Gas Mark 6.

2. When you're ready to cook the pork, rub a little oil over the skin and then rub in a generous amount of sea salt on top of the skin and into the score lines.

3. Cut the onions in half and sit in a roasting tray cut-side up with a trickle of oil. Place the pork on top and cook for 20 minutes before reducing the heat to 180°C/350°F/

Gas Mark 4 and cooking for a further 1 hour 20 minutes. There is no need to baste the pork during cooking as the skin does the job for you, keeping the meat moist as it becomes crisp.

4. When the pork is cooked, remove from the tray and sit on a plate in a warm place to rest. Remove the onions from the tray and keep warm with the pork, then pour out any excess fat. Put the tray over a medium heat

and stir the flour vigorously into the meat juices. Slowly add the mustard, cider and vegetable stock and cook for about 3–4 minutes until thickened slightly. Finally add the cream, if using, and season with salt and pepper.

5. Remove the crackling from the pork and break into pieces. Thickly slice the pork and serve with the onions, gravy and sauce.

Apple, Pear and Sage Sauce

- 40 g (1½ oz) butter
- 350 g (12 oz) Bramley apples, peeled, cored and cut into small chunks
- 350 g (12 oz) ripe pears, peeled, cored and cut into small chunks
- 2 teaspoons caster sugar

- 50 ml (2 fl oz) cider or apple juice
- 1 tablespoon finely chopped sage leaves

1. Place the butter, apples, pears, sugar and cider or apple juice in a saucepan and bring to a simmer. Cover with a lid

and cook for about 10–15 minutes or until the fruits have softened and are beginning to purée. Remove from the heat and stir in the sage. The sauce can now be stirred briskly for a smoother texture or left fairly chunky.

=5

Baked Potato

We all thought the Irish liked their spuds. But only one per cent of the people of Northern Ireland chose a baked potato for their lunch, compared to the North East of England where it is twenty times more popular. Although only joint fifth in the favourite lunch section, it was actually voted second favourite for a weekday lunch.

You can bake a potato quickly in the microwave but there's nothing to beat one cooked in the oven with a crispy skin and soft, fluffy inside.

The Perfect Baked Potato

- 1 fat, floury potato per person (Maris Piper, King Edward or Marfona are all good bakers)
- olive oil
- flaked sea salt

1. Pre-heat the oven to 200°C/400°F/Gas Mark 6.

2. Wash the potatoes well, dry them and prick several times with a fork. Pour some olive oil into your hands and rub over the potatoes, then scatter over some sea salt which should stick to the oil. Place directly on the shelf in the oven and bake for a good $1^{1}/_{4}$–$1^{1}/_{2}$ hours, depending on the size of the potato. When cooked, the potato should be golden and crispy on the outside and give a little when squeezed. Serve split open with lots of salted butter or try one of the suggestions opposite.

Gratinated Smoked Trout Filling   Serves 2

- 2 baked potatoes
- 2 fillets of smoked trout
- 1 tablespoon chopped parsley or chives
- 2 handfuls of grated mature Cheddar cheese
- 1 teaspoon hot horseradish sauce or English mustard
- 2 large knobs of butter
- flaked sea salt and freshly ground black pepper

1. Pre-heat the grill to medium-high.

2. Split the baked potatoes in half and scoop out most of the fluffy flesh with a fork into a bowl. Flake in the trout and add the parsley or chives, three-quarters of the cheese, the horseradish or mustard and butter.

3. Season with salt and pepper and then lightly mix together. Spoon back into the potato skins, sit on a baking sheet and scatter over the remaining cheese. Grill until the cheese is bubbling and the filling is becoming golden in places.

Curried Cream Cheese Topping   Serves 2

- 2 baked potatoes
- 150 g (5 oz) cream cheese
- 1 tablespoon medium curry paste
- 4 spring onions or 1/2 small red onion, chopped
- approx 2.5 cm (1 in) piece of cucumber, cut into dice
- 1–2 ripe tomatoes, chopped
- a small handful of mint or coriander leaves, roughly chopped
- good squeeze of lemon or lime juice
- flaked sea salt and freshly ground black pepper

1. Mix together all of the ingredients, except the baked potatoes, and season with salt and pepper.

2. Split open the cooked potatoes and spoon the cheese mixture on top: it will melt and ooze into the hot, steaming potato.

TIP
Try adding the following to the curried cream cheese:
- 1 tablespoon mango chutney for a sweet touch
- cooked prawns or shredded cooked chicken
- chopped hard-boiled egg
- sultanas soaked in a little warm water for 10 minutes
- roasted peanuts or cashew nuts

7

Soup

Soup is all things to all people and, just like people, it has many personalities. The hail-fellow-well-met soup is a hearty, beany broth to be enjoyed on a frosty winter's day; the funky-chatty-chick soup is spicy Thai coconut; while the Aunt Marjorie of soups is the summer chilled consommé with a swirl of yoghurt and a few snipped chives. Whatever your personality, age or location, the recipe below is a really good all-rounder. Or see page 108 for a classic Creamy Tomato Soup.

Leek, Gorgonzola and Rosemary Soup   Serves 4–6

- 4 sprigs of rosemary
- 2 tablespoons olive oil
- 2 medium potatoes, peeled and cut into cubes
- 4 medium-sized leeks, sliced
- 2 cloves of garlic, crushed
- 1.2 litres (2 pints) hot vegetable stock
- 200 g (7 oz) Gorgonzola cheese, roughly chopped
- $\frac{1}{2}$ –1 teaspoon Dijon mustard
- flaked sea salt and freshly ground black pepper
- bread, to serve

1. Lightly bash the rosemary stalks with a rolling pin to help release the powerful aroma and flavour when cooking.

2. Heat the oil in a saucepan and stir in the potatoes and rosemary. Cover with a lid and cook on a low heat for 4–5 minutes. This will create some steam in the pan, preventing the potatoes from sticking to the base. Stir in the leeks and garlic, then cook for a couple of minutes until beginning to soften. Add the stock and bring to a simmer, leaving it to cook for 10 minutes.

3. Remove from the heat, take out the rosemary stalks and stir in the Gorgonzola cheese and Dijon mustard. It doesn't matter if the cheese doesn't melt completely as you now need to place the soup into a blender or food processor and blitz until smooth.

4. Season with salt and pepper, making sure you taste the soup first as Gorgonzola is quite a salty cheese. If the consistency seems too thick, add some extra vegetable stock to loosen.

5. Serve with some fresh bread while the soup is still hot – walnut bread is really nice – or if you're not eating it straight away, gently reheat, being careful not to let it boil as this will give the soup a grainy texture.

8   Toasted Sandwich

More women than men like a toastie for lunch; in particular, those in the North East of England and Wales. Make the most of the wonderful breads available these days. The recipe below is the kind of sandwich you'd order in an Italian coffee shop, but it can easily be made in a toasted sandwich machine with white sliced bread if you prefer.

Tricolore Italian Toastie   Serves 2, generously

- 1 medium round focaccia, flavoured or plain
- a good dollop of green pesto
- 1 ball of mozzarella cheese, sliced
- 4–6 slices of Parma ham (optional)
- 1 small ripe avocado, peeled, stoned and sliced
- 2 ripe tomatoes, sliced
- salt and freshly ground black pepper
- olive oil

1. Place a ridged or plain grill plate over a low heat.

2. Slice the focaccia bread through the middle into 2 rounds. Spread both of the cut sides with pesto and place the mozzarella, Parma ham (if using), avocado and tomatoes on the cut side of one piece of bread. Season with salt and pepper. Firmly press the other half of the bread on top and sit on the grill plate. The bread should be fairly oily on the outside so you shouldn't need to add any oil to the grill plate. However, you can brush the grill with some olive oil if you feel it needs it. Leave to cook for about 8 minutes, pressing down with a fish slice every so often until the bread has become golden on the base. Carefully turn over and repeat until the second side is golden and the filling is hot, with the cheese beginning to ooze out at the sides. Serve the sandwich straight away, cut into wedges.

9 Pasta with Sauce

Wales appears to be the lunchtime pasta capital of Britain, with 18 per cent of the population voting it their top choice during the week.

This basic sauce can be adapted in a variety of ways (see below) and is perfect for a light lunch.

Basic Tomato and Basil Sauce for Pasta
Serves 6

- 3 tablespoons extra-virgin olive oil
- 1 large onion, chopped
- 2 cloves of garlic, crushed
- 3 x 400 g (14 oz) tins of chopped tomatoes
- $\frac{1}{4}$–$\frac{1}{2}$ teaspoon dried chilli flakes
- 2 teaspoons balsamic vinegar
- 2 teaspoons sugar
- 1 large handful of basil leaves, torn into small pieces
- salt and freshly ground black pepper
- grated Parmesan cheese, to serve

1. Heat the oil in a saucepan and gently cook the onion and garlic until softened. Stir in the tomatoes, chilli flakes, balsamic vinegar and sugar. Bring to a simmer and cook slowly for 45 minutes–1 hour. Stir in the basil and season with salt and pepper. This can be left chunky or blended in a food processor for a smooth sauce.

Serve spooned over cooked pasta with plenty of Parmesan cheese.

This is a perfect sauce to use as a base. You can add a variety of other flavours to the finished sauce, just cooking for a few minutes to create a completely different dish:

- 250 g (9 oz) tub of mascarpone or cream cheese, either alone or with strips of smoked salmon
- chopped black olives and marinated artichokes
- fried bacon and mushrooms
- prawns, capers and chopped parsley
- chopped chicken, red onion and red peppers, fried in olive oil
- fried slices of chorizo sausage, chopped black olives and pieces of mozzarella cheese

10 Baked Beans on Toast

In 1928 the Heinz baked bean tin arrived on our grocery store shelves and gave us one of the most convenient store-cupboard foods ever invented. Share this version with your friends for a satisfying and original lunchtime snack.

Baked Bean Bake
Serves 2–3

- thick slices of brown or white bread
- 1 onion, chopped
- olive oil
- 2 x 415 g (14$\frac{1}{2}$ oz) tins of baked beans
- Tabasco sauce
- Worcestershire sauce
- freshly ground black pepper
- butter, for spreading
- 100 g (4 oz) Cheddar cheese, grated

1. Pre-heat the oven to 180°C/350°F/Gas Mark 4.

2. Lightly toast the bread either under the grill or in a toaster. Fry the onion in a little olive oil until just becoming golden.

3. Place the baked beans in a shallow ovenproof dish and stir in the onion. For extra flavour and an additional kick to the beans, mix in a few good shakes of Tabasco and Worcestershire sauce and plenty of freshly ground black pepper. If these don't tickle your fancy, try some of the suggestions below, or add your own favourite twist.

4. Spread the toast with butter and cut each slice into 4 triangles. Place buttered-side up on top of the beans, overlapping each piece until the surface is covered. Scatter over the cheese and bake in the oven for about 20 minutes until golden and bubbling.

TIP
Add any of the following combinations to this recipe or to spice up plain and simple baked beans on toast:
- **2–3 chopped fresh tomatoes**
- **strips of ham or fried bacon**
- **fried mushrooms**
- **$\frac{1}{2}$ teaspoon garam masala or curry powder**
- **fresh or dried herbs**
- **1 teaspoon English or Dijon mustard**
- **tomato ketchup**
- **sweet chilli sauce**

3:
Nation's Favourite
Dinner

Ninety-four per cent of people surveyed said they ate their main meal in the evening. This might be a reflection of our changing lifestyles, suggesting we're all too busy to partake of a decent meal during the day, and instead rely on something we can grab and eat in the shortest time possible.

And the nation's favourite dinner is another reflection of our changing lifestyles. We all know the British diet has been influenced by many other cultures, and it's the Italians who've given us the most popular dish: spaghetti Bolognese. In fact, pasta and rice have overtaken potatoes as the main form of carbohydrate in our diet and you only have to look at the list of top ten dinners to realize there are very few dishes that originated in this country.

Curry is really no surprise – you may remember the first packet curry by Vesta in 1961 where you simply added water to create an instant meal. It wasn't in the slightest bit authentic but it gave us a taste of an exotic food we knew little about. The rise of the Indian restaurant has confirmed our love for this spicy, flavoursome food and the curry is now a great 'British' tradition.

In the 1980s Ken Hom hit our TV screens and introduced us to a cooking implement that revolutionized our attitude to home cooking: the wok. Stir-fry was voted in at number seven. Nigel Slater argues that you can't make a successful stir-fry at home as you need Olympic-sized flames to cook the food in the right way: 'To stir-fry properly you have got to be a bit scared. You've got to think, "Oh my God, this is going to blow up in my face, because there's so much heat." So standing there over a domestic cooker with your wok and your little doll's-house stirrer, the second you put anything in it the heat's gone. You end up with a stew-fry instead.'

Another favourite, the chilli con carne, is thought to be a Mexican dish, but in fact originates in North America. We seem to have adopted it as our own, serving it up with guacamole, sour cream, grated cheese and taco chips. The veggie version is just as popular, using a variety of vegetables instead of minced meat.

Easier access to unusual ingredients and a wealth of TV cookery shows have made us much more adventurous in the kitchen. But, according to Gordon Ramsay, we shouldn't be trying to emulate the TV chefs or the Michelin-starred restaurant meal when we're cooking for people at home: 'We become lunatics because we believe it's a gastronomic event. We know full well no matter what we have to eat and how things look, it's the flavour that holds the memory. Ninety-nine per cent of the dinner parties I've been to, they're slightly pissed because they can't cope with the pressure. Why put yourself under scrutiny? Relax, simplify your food, don't push the boundaries out, you've got nothing to prove. Do what the missus does and bring out a cottage pie. Lovely wine, lovely salad, everybody's happy.'

So Mrs Ramsay makes a cottage pie, but where are all the other great British dishes? Sausage and mash was number 12, steak and kidney pie wasn't even in the top 20, and Lancashire hotpot only scored two per cent of the votes. But the traditional roast meat and two veg is in there at number five – not so great for vegetarians, though. Next time your veggie friends come round for dinner, forget the nut roast; try a dish like the butternut risotto on page 51 – after all, vegetarians have taste buds too.

1

Spaghetti Bolognese

Spag Bol, as it's affectionately known, is most popular in Wales where over a quarter of those who voted made it their top dinner. *Ragù* is the true name for the Bolognese sauce that's served with lasagne verdi rather than spaghetti in its home town of Bologna, and includes chicken livers, bacon, carrot and celery. The sun-dried tomatoes and marinated mushrooms in this version give the sauce a distinctive taste and a really rich flavour; it tastes even better the day after you make it!

Spaghetti Bolognese   Serves 6–8

- 2 tablespoons olive oil or sun-dried tomato oil from the jar
- 6 rashers of smoked streaky bacon, chopped
- 2 large onions, chopped
- 3 cloves of garlic, crushed
- 1 kg (2¼ lb) lean minced beef
- 2 large glasses of red wine
- 2 x 14 oz (400 g) tins of chopped tomatoes
- 1 jar (290 g) of antipasti marinated mushrooms, drained
- 2 fresh or dried bay leaves

- 1 teaspoon dried oregano or a small handful of fresh leaves, chopped
- 1 teaspoon dried thyme or a small handful of fresh leaves, chopped
- drizzle of balsamic vinegar
- 12–14 sun-dried tomato halves, in oil
- salt and freshly ground black pepper
- a good handful of fresh basil leaves, torn into small pieces
- 800 g–1 kg (1¾–2¼ lb) dried spaghetti
- lots of freshly grated Parmesan cheese, to serve

1. Heat the oil in a large, heavy-based saucepan and fry the bacon until golden over a medium heat. Add the onions and garlic, frying until softened. Increase the heat and add the minced beef. Fry it until it has browned, breaking down any chunks of meat with a wooden spoon. Pour in the wine and boil until it has reduced in volume by about a third. Reduce the temperature and stir in the tomatoes, drained mushrooms, bay leaves, oregano, thyme and balsamic vinegar.

2. Either blitz the sun-dried tomatoes in a small blender with a little of the oil to loosen, or just finely chop before adding to the pan. Season well with salt and pepper. Cover with a lid and simmer the Bolognese sauce over a gentle heat for 1–1½ hours until it's rich and thickened, stirring

occasionally. At the end of the cooking time, stir in the basil and add any extra seasoning if necessary.

3. Remove from the heat to 'settle' while you cook the spaghetti in plenty of boiling salted water (for the time stated on the packet). Drain and divide between warmed plates. Scatter a little Parmesan over the spaghetti before adding a good ladleful of the Bolognese sauce, finishing with a scattering of more cheese and a twist of black pepper.

TIP
You can make a veggie version of this recipe by substituting soya mince or Quorn for the meat, adding it to the sauce halfway through cooking. Or simply add lots of diced vegetables to the onions, such as courgettes, carrots, peppers and aubergines.

2 Curry with Rice

There's such a huge array of curries to choose from nowadays, from the once-top-of-the-list Indian chicken tikka masala, to Thai, Indonesian, Chinese and Vietnamese curries. Whatever the variety, more men than women voted curry in at number two, and it's almost as popular with vegetarians as it is with meat-eaters.

Simple Goan Chicken Curry

- 4 large skinless chicken breasts, cut into chunks
- 3 tablespoons vegetable oil
- 1 teaspoon yellow or brown mustard seeds
- 1 large onion, sliced
- 3 cloves of garlic, finely sliced
- 400 ml (14 fl oz) tin of coconut milk
- salt

MARINADE
- 1 teaspoon paprika
- ½ teaspoon ground turmeric
- 1½ tablespoons ground coriander
- 1 teaspoon ground cumin
- 1 teaspoon cayenne pepper
- 1 tablespoon lemon juice
- ½ teaspoon salt
- 75 ml (2¾ fl oz) water

1. Mix together all the marinade ingredients to give you a loose, smooth paste. Add the chicken pieces and coat them in the paste. They are best left to marinate for around 30 minutes–1 hour, but if you're in a hurry a few minutes will do.

2. Heat the oil in a deep frying pan and add the mustard seeds. When they start to pop and jump about in the pan, add the onion and garlic. Cook until they're golden brown before adding the chicken and any extra paste from the marinade. Fry over a gentle heat for about 8 minutes before adding the coconut milk. Increase the heat slightly and bring to a simmer. Cook for a further 10–12 minutes until the sauce has thickened slightly before seasoning with salt if necessary and serving with Fragrant Pilau Rice or naan bread.

Fragrant Pilau Rice

- 450 g (1 lb) basmati rice (for a more authentic flavour and texture it's best not to use 'easy-cook' rice; however, it will still work and be very tasty if you do)
- 1 medium onion, finely chopped
- large knob of butter, plus extra to serve
- 4 cardamom pods
- 8 cloves
- 1 cinnamon stick
- pinch of saffron threads
- 2 bay leaves
- 600 ml (1 pint) hot chicken stock, vegetable stock or water
- salt

1. To make sure you get lovely fluffy rice, wash it in several changes of cold water, then leave to soak for about 30 minutes in fresh cold water. If you don't have time for this, place in a sieve and wash under the cold tap for a minute or so.

2. Cook the onion in the butter for around 5 minutes until softened. Add the spices, saffron and bay leaves and cook for a couple more minutes. The spices will give a wonderful fragrant flavour to the rice. Add the rice and stir until the grains are coated in the butter before stirring in the stock or water and salt. Bring to the boil and then cover with a tight-fitting lid. If the lid isn't very tight, cover the pan with aluminium foil before putting the lid on. Turn the heat down low and leave to cook for 10 minutes before turning off the heat. Don't remove the lid; just leave the rice to continue cooking in the pan for about 5 minutes until you're ready to serve.

3. The rice should have absorbed all the water and will just need fluffing up with a fork. Add a knob of butter before serving.

3

Fried or Grilled Fish

Fish for dinner used to mean a trip down to the chip shop on a Friday night. Maybe that's why fried or grilled fish is more popular with the over-55s, and with men in particular. But it's not a dish favoured by the Welsh: only five per cent of them voted it their favourite evening meal.

The recipe below is great for dinner parties – the fish can be prepared in advance and popped under the grill ten minutes before you're ready to eat.

Gremolata Grilled Salmon with Oven-roasted Tomatoes and Lemon

- 8 ripe plum tomatoes, cut in half
- 2 cloves of garlic, chopped
- 1 teaspoon caster sugar
- flaked sea salt and freshly ground black pepper
- extra-virgin olive oil
- 1 large lemon, cut into 4 wedges
- 1 heaped tablespoon capers, drained
- 2 large handfuls of flat-leaf parsley, roughly chopped
- grated zest of 1 lemon
- 8 green olives, pitted
- 4 thick salmon fillets, approx. 200 g (7 oz) each, skinned

1. Pre-heat the oven to 200°C/400°F/Gas Mark 6 and the grill to medium.

2. With a small, sharp knife, remove the green 'eye' from the tomatoes as this is tough and bitter to eat. Sit the tomatoes cut-side up in a roasting tray, then scatter over the chopped garlic and caster sugar and season with salt and pepper. Pour over a generous drizzle of olive oil and sit the lemon wedges next to the tomatoes. Roast in the oven for about 25 minutes until the tomatoes are rich and juicy and the lemon wedges are golden and caramelized. By roasting the lemon wedges you get a sweeter-flavoured juice to squeeze over the cooked salmon.

3. To make the gremolata, place the capers, parsley, lemon zest, olives, about 2 tablespoons olive oil and plenty of salt and pepper in a pestle and mortar, then pound to a rough paste. Alternatively, blitz briefly in a small food processor, or finely chop the capers, parsley, lemon zest and olives together, then mix with the oil and seasoning.

4. Spread the gremolata over the top of the salmon fillets and sit on a baking tray brushed with a little oil to stop the salmon sticking. Place under the grill for 7–8 minutes until just cooked through.

5. Serve the salmon with the roasted tomatoes and a roasted lemon wedge to squeeze over. All that's needed is a green salad to complete the dish and to complement the colours of the salmon and tomatoes.

4   Seafood

**Mussels, crab, scallops, lobster, and prawns: we have a wealth of
seafood in this country, and when fresh they're some of the best flavours
in the world.** As we begin to understand and appreciate our own country's
natural resources we learn how to include such things as seafood in our
weekly diet. Those in the Midlands and Northern Ireland are three times
more likely to serve seafood at a dinner party than their fellow
countrymen in Wales and Scotland.

For an informal dinner-party dish, this seafood broth is a delight to
share with friends – just pass round hunks of fresh crusty bread to dunk
in the sauce.

Saucy Seafood Broth   Serves 6

- 1.5 kg (3 lb) fresh raw mixed seafood – mussels, clams, scallops, tiger prawns, squid rings
- extra-virgin olive oil
- 1 large onion, sliced
- 4 cloves of garlic, chopped
- 2 red chillies, de-seeded and finely chopped, or 2–3 teaspoons dried chilli flakes
- 300 ml (10 fl oz) bottle of dry cider
- 400 g (14 oz) tin of chopped tomatoes
- 2 tablespoons tomato purée
- 1 heaped tablespoon capers, drained
- flaked sea salt and freshly ground black pepper
- a large handful of mixed fresh herbs (e.g. parsley, basil, chives, chervil), chopped
- 1 lemon, cut into wedges
- fresh crusty bread, to serve

1. Before you start cooking, prepare the seafood. Remove any beardy bits from the mussels and wash them with the clams in plenty of cold water. Remove the heads and shells from the prawns, ideally leaving the tails on for a more attractive look to the finished dish. The scallops and squid rings can be left as they are.

2. Pour a couple of generous glugs of olive oil into a large pan. Once it is hot, add the onion, garlic and chillies or chilli flakes and cook over a medium heat until the onion has softened. Increase the heat and add the prepared mussels and clams and the cider. Boil for 1 minute, then shake around in the pan before adding the tinned tomatoes, tomato purée, capers and remaining seafood. Cover with a lid and cook for about 5 minutes, until all of the shellfish are open and the prawns are pink.

3. Season well with salt and pepper, then add the herbs. Remove any seafood shells that haven't opened as these shouldn't be eaten, then ladle into big bowls and serve with a wedge of lemon and lots of crusty bread.

A few lemon wedges in a bowl of warm water placed on the table after the broth has been devoured allows everyone to rinse their fishy fingers.

5

Roast Dinner and All the Trimmings

It would appear that if you live in the South West of England you're fourteen times more likely to choose a traditional roast for dinner than if you live in Wales. But it's a dish that's popular with all age groups; this roast lamb makes a great centrepiece at a dinner party.

Roast Lemon and Thyme Lamb with Redcurrant Madeira Gravy   Serves 6 generously

- 6–8 sprigs of thyme, cut into pieces (leave a couple whole)
- 3 red onions, cut in half
- peeled zest of 1 large lemon, cut into pieces
- 1 bulb of garlic, cut in half across the centre
- 1 leg of lamb, about 2 kg (4½ lb)
- olive oil
- salt and freshly ground black pepper
- 2 tablespoons redcurrant jelly
- 175 ml (6 fl oz) Madeira wine
- 350 ml (12 fl oz) lamb stock or water

1. Pre-heat the oven to 220°C/425°F/Gas Mark 7.

2. Place the whole sprigs of thyme, the onions, half the lemon zest and the halved garlic in a roasting tray with 4 tablespoons water and sit the lamb on top. Randomly insert a small sharp knife into the fatty surface of the lamb, twisting to create small holes. Stuff sprigs of thyme and the remaining lemon zest into the holes, then drizzle and rub over a little olive oil. Season well with salt and pepper and place in the oven for 20 minutes.

3. Reduce the oven temperature to 200°C/400°F/Gas Mark 6 and spoon any juices from the tray over the lamb. Cook for a further 1 hour for medium lamb, spooning the juices over a couple of times during the cooking. If you don't like your lamb pink, leave for a further 15–20 minutes for medium–well done.

4. Once it is cooked, remove the lamb and place on to a warm plate or carving board to 'relax'. Pour away any excess fat from the roasting tray, then sit the tray on the hob over a high heat. Stir the redcurrant jelly into the roasted onions and garlic until melted before adding the Madeira wine. Boil for about 30 seconds and add the stock or water. Bring to a simmer and cook for a couple of minutes until thickened slightly, then season with salt and pepper. Strain through a sieve to give you a rich, loose gravy.

Minty Lemon Roast Potatoes   Serves 6

- 8–10 large floury potatoes, such as King Edward, peeled and cut into chunks, depending on how big you like them
- grated zest of 1 lemon
- lard, fat from the roast or vegetable oil
- flaked sea salt
- a handful of mint leaves, chopped

1. Pre-heat the oven to 200°C/400°F/Gas Mark 6.

2. Place the potatoes in a large saucepan of cold salted water. Bring to the boil and cook for 5–6 minutes. Drain and sprinkle over the lemon zest. Shake lightly in the colander to fluff up the outside of the potatoes and give a crunchy finish when roasted.

3. Tip the potatoes into a shallow roasting tray with enough hot lard, fat or vegetable oil to cover the base. Roll the potatoes in the fat and roast, turning occasionally, for about 45 minutes–1 hour, depending on how small they are cut or how crispy you like them. Pour away any excess fat and sprinkle over plenty of sea salt. For additional crispness, return to the oven for a few minutes before scattering over the chopped mint.

Serve with the roast lamb, gravy and perhaps some thin green beans. If runners are in season, there's no better combination.

You can also serve this with Mint Sauce (see page 152).

6

Chilli con Carne

Chilli is particularly popular at opposite ends of the country. Twice as many voted it their favourite in the North East and South West than in London, where only seven per cent said they preferred it as an evening meal. Now red kidney beans are available ready cooked in a tin it saves endless soaking of the dried variety overnight, and the tinned ones taste almost as good.

Chilli con Carne Serves 6–8

- 2 tablespoons olive oil
- 2 onions, chopped
- 2 cloves of garlic, crushed
- 1 kg (2¼ lb) lean minced beef
- 2 glasses of red wine
- 2 x 400 g (14 oz) tins of chopped tomatoes
- 3 tablespoons tomato purée
- 2 red chillies, thinly sliced, or 3–4 teaspoons dried chilli flakes
- 1 teaspoon ground cumin
- 1 teaspoon ground coriander
- 1 stick of cinnamon
- good shake of Worcestershire sauce
- 1 beef stock cube
- salt and freshly ground black pepper
- 2 x 400 g (14 oz) tins of red kidney beans, drained
- 1 large bunch of coriander leaves, roughly chopped
- wedges of lime, to serve

1. Heat the oil in a large, heavy-based saucepan and fry the onion and garlic until softened. Increase the heat and add the mince, cooking quickly until browned and breaking down any chunks of meat with a wooden spoon. Pour in the red wine and boil for 2–3 minutes. While waiting, pour a glass for yourself.

2. Stir in the tinned tomatoes, tomato purée, fresh chilli or chilli flakes, cumin, ground coriander, cinnamon, and Worcestershire sauce and crumble in the stock cube. Season well with salt and pepper. Bring to a simmer, cover with a lid and cook over a gentle heat for about 50 minutes–1 hour, stirring occasionally until the mixture is rich and thickened. Add the kidney beans and fresh coriander. Cook for a further 10 minutes, uncovered, before removing from the heat, adding any extra seasoning if necessary. This is ideal served with the lime wedges and also rice, crusty bread or jacket potatoes, guacamole, sour cream and a big green salad.

TIPS

The chilli is much tastier a day or two after it's cooked as the flavours develop and the texture becomes richer. Simply leave to cool, stick in the fridge and gently heat before serving. If you're eating the chilli on the day you prepared it, any leftovers can be frozen in individual portions in well-sealed sandwich bags, then reheated by boiling from frozen in a saucepan of water for about 15–20 minutes until steaming hot.

7

Stir-fry

If you're under 25 you're much more likely to choose stir-fry for dinner.
And the older you get, the less you like it. For the novice stir-fry eater this
might sound like an adventurous recipe, but you can adjust almost all the
ingredients to suit your taste buds. If you can't get hold of pak choi or
Chinese flowering cabbage, just use baby spinach leaves or finely
shredded white, green or red cabbage. And remember Nigel Slater's
advice: keep the heat high so you don't end up with a stew-fry instead.

Spicy Prawn Stir-fry

- 500 g (1 lb 2 oz) medium
  egg noodles
- 2 tablespoons sesame
  oil, plus extra for tossing
  the noodles
- 2 red chillies, de-seeded
  and finely chopped
- thumb-size piece of
  fresh ginger, peeled and
  finely chopped
- 3 large cloves of garlic,
  chopped
- 1 red pepper, de-seeded
  and thinly sliced
- 1 bunch of spring
  onions, thinly sliced on
  an angle
- 400 g (14 oz) raw tiger
  prawns, shelled
- 2 large or 3 small pak
  choi, or 200 g (7 oz)
  Chinese flowering
  cabbage (choi sum),
  shredded
- juice of 1 lime
- 2 tablespoons soy sauce
- 2 tablespoons sweet
  chilli sauce
- 100 ml (3½ fl oz)
  Chinese rice wine or dry
  sherry

1. Cook the noodles
according to the
instructions given on the
packet. Drain and toss in a
little sesame oil to
prevent them from
sticking together.

2. Heat a wok and add the
sesame oil. Once the oil is
shimmering, add the
chillies, ginger and garlic.
Stir-fry for 30 seconds
before adding the red
pepper, spring onions and
shelled prawns. Cook for
about 3–4 minutes until
the prawns have turned
pink. Add the shredded
pak choi or choi sum,
noodles, lime juice, soy
sauce, sweet chilli sauce
and rice wine or sherry.
Stir-fry until heated
through and serve
straight away.

8 Stuffed Chicken Breast

Chicken Kiev – a whole breast bursting with hot garlic butter – is probably what inspired people to vote for this as their favourite dinner dish. Chicken breast is five times more popular in the North West of England than it is in Scotland, where only four per cent said they'd choose it for dinner. This recipe uses some classic Italian ingredients to turn the stuffed chicken breast into a delicious, succulent dish. The summery flavours will add a ray of sunshine to any evening meal.

Stuffed Chicken in a Parma Parcel

- 2 tablespoons sun-dried tomato oil, from the jar
- 1 small red onion, chopped
- 2 cloves of garlic, crushed
- 120 g (4$\frac{1}{2}$ oz) chestnut mushrooms, finely chopped
- 2 balls of mozzarella cheese, preferably Buffalo, grated or torn into small pieces
- 8 sun-dried tomato halves, chopped
- a handful of grated Parmesan cheese
- flaked sea salt and freshly ground black pepper
- a handful of basil leaves, torn
- 4 skinless, boneless chicken breasts
- 8 slices of Parma ham
- 4 stalks of rosemary or 8 cocktail sticks
- balsamic vinegar
- roast new potatoes (see step 5 of method) and green salad, to serve

1. Pre-heat the oven to 200°C/400°F/Gas Mark 6.

2. Heat about 1 tablespoon of the sun-dried tomato oil in a frying pan. Add the onion and garlic, then gently fry for a few minutes until softened. Stir in the mushrooms, also cooking until softened. Remove from the heat and leave to cool for a few minutes.

3. In a bowl, mix together the mozzarella, sun-dried tomatoes, Parmesan cheese and the cooked mushroom mixture and season well with salt and pepper. Add the basil and mix together well.

4. Slice the chicken breasts along the centre lengthways, not quite cutting all the way through, and open out to form a butterfly shape. Divide the mozzarella mixture between the chicken breasts and fold back together pushing any escaped stuffing inside. Wrap each breast fairly tightly in 2 slices of Parma ham and either secure with a couple of cocktail sticks or use rosemary stalks pushed through, which also add extra flavour to the finished chicken.

5. Place the parcels in a roasting tray, drizzle with the remaining sun-dried tomato oil and season with pepper. Cook for 18–20 minutes until golden and cooked through. Remove from the oven and allow to rest for a couple of minutes before serving. Pour over any juices from the pan and drizzle with a little balsamic vinegar. Serve with new potatoes roasted in the oven, also at 200°C/400°F/Gas Mark 6, with rosemary, olive oil and sea salt for about 25 minutes, and a big green salad.

9   Risotto

Once a great way of using up the leftovers in the fridge, risotto has now become a sophisticated dish that would work just as well for a midweek supper as it would for an informal dinner party. The secret is to keep it simple and not be tempted to throw in an extra handful of peas or some diced red pepper to pretty it up. The Italians' idea of a perfect risotto is just good rice, stock and freshly grated Parmesan cheese. The principle is exactly the same for this recipe – some good raw ingredients, hot stock, and lots and lots of stirring.

Roasted Butternut Squash and Sage Risotto with Pinenuts

- 1 large butternut squash
- 2 cloves of garlic, peeled
- 2 tablespoons olive oil, plus extra for drizzling
- about 15 sage leaves, chopped
- flaked sea salt and freshly ground black pepper
- 3 large knobs of butter
- 1 large onion, chopped
- 400 g (14 oz) Arborio or other Italian risotto rice
- 2 glasses of white wine
- about 1 litre (1³/₄ pints) hot chicken or vegetable stock
- a good handful of freshly grated Parmesan cheese, plus extra to serve
- 75 g (3 oz) pinenuts, to serve

1. Pre-heat the oven to 200°C/400°F/Gas Mark 6.

2. Cut the butternut squash into 6–8 wedges, remove the seeds and place in a roasting tray. Pound or chop the garlic and add a generous glug of olive oil, half the sage leaves, sea salt and pepper. Tip into the tray and rub over the butternut squash with your hands. Roast in the oven for 40–50 minutes until softened and becoming golden in colour.

3. Once the squash has cooked, cool slightly, then scrape the soft flesh away from the skin into a bowl. Lightly mash with a fork or potato masher until it is fairly chunky in texture. Scrape any sticky juices left in the roasting tray into the bowl and keep warm while making the risotto.

4. Heat the 2 tablespoons of olive oil and a good knob of butter in a deep, heavy-based frying pan or sauté pan. Gently fry the onion until softened. Add the rice and stir for about a minute until the grains are coated with the oil and butter. Pour in the wine and stir continuously until it has cooked into the rice. Add a good ladle of hot stock and the remaining sage and season well with salt and pepper. Turn the heat down so the stock is simmering gently. Keep adding ladles of stock as it cooks into the rice, stirring and moving the rice around in the pan. After about 15-20 minutes the rice should be soft but still have a bit of bite left in it. The texture of the risotto should be thick and creamy, but not too loose. Add extra stock if necessary. It may seem tedious standing and stirring but the end result will be worth it.

5. Remove the pan from the heat and gently stir the roasted butternut squash into the risotto with the Parmesan, the remaining butter and seasoning to taste. Add any extra stock if the risotto seems particularly thick. Cover with a lid for a couple of minutes as this will give the risotto an even creamier texture.

6. During this time, place the pinenuts in a fairly hot frying pan and toss around until golden. Spoon the risotto into warmed bowls and scatter with the pinenuts and extra Parmesan.

TIP

For a smoky finish to the risotto, fry 6–8 slices of smoked streaky bacon cut into thin strips or 200 g (7 oz) lardons until crispy and scatter over the risotto with the pinenuts.

10 Duck with Sauce

Although nearly nine per cent of the population voted this in at number ten, 14 per cent of the over-55s said they preferred duck for a dinner party. To get away from the traditional duck *à l'orange* or with wild cherry sauce, this duck breast has an oriental flavour and should appeal to the younger generation as well. It looks fantastically impressive and is far easier to serve than a whole duck at the table.

Really Crispy Duck Breast with Chinese-style Cranberry Sauce

- 1 tablespoon sesame oil
- 1 red onion, thinly sliced
- 2 cm (³/₄ in) piece of fresh ginger, peeled and finely chopped or grated
- 1 tablespoon red wine vinegar
- 4 tablespoons cranberry sauce
- 1¹/₂ teaspoons Chinese five spice
- 1 large glass of red wine
- 1 peeled strip of orange zest
- juice of ¹/₂ orange
- 1 teaspoon brown sugar
- coarse sea salt and freshly ground black pepper
- 4 thick duck breasts
- vegetable oil

1. The sauce can be prepared while the duck's cooking, or made well in advance and warmed just before serving. Heat the sesame oil in a small saucepan and cook the onion until softened. Add the ginger and red wine vinegar. Bring to the boil and cook until the vinegar has almost cooked away. Stir in the cranberry sauce, ¹/₂ teaspoon of the Chinese five spice, the red wine, orange zest, orange juice and sugar. Bring to the boil and cook for 6–8 minutes until thickened slightly. Season with salt and remove the orange zest before serving.

2. Pre-heat the oven to 200°C/400°F/Gas Mark 6.

3. Score the skin of the duck breasts several times with a sharp knife. Sprinkle over the remaining Chinese five spice, salt and pepper, then rub into the skin and score lines.

4. Heat a drop of vegetable oil in an ovenproof frying pan or roasting tray over a low–medium heat. Sit the duck skin-side down in the pan or tray and slowly fry for 10–12 minutes. Be patient at this stage as it will give you a really crispy skin as a result. Drain away all the excess fat. Turn the breasts over so they are skin-side up, and cook in the oven for 6–8 minutes (you may need a couple of minutes longer if the breasts are very thick).

5. Remove from the oven and leave to relax for about 5 minutes. This will ensure the duck breasts are tender while still keeping the skin crispy. The duck is now ready to serve on warm plates with a spoonful of sauce and accompaniment of your choice. Try some stir-fried spinach or pak choi with sesame oil, and noodles or mashed potatoes flavoured with thinly sliced spring onions.

4:
Nation's Favourite
Food of Love

It's official – if you want to get your partner in the mood for love, you couldn't do better than serve up strawberries and cream, the nation's biggest turn-on. We all know that oysters, champagne, asparagus and chocolate are supposed to help promote sexual desire, yet the strawberry is in a league of its own as a sexy food.

Fruits are often a first choice for erotic pleasure. The texture and sweetness of a ripe fig was Cleopatra's favourite, and the ancient Greeks celebrated the midsummer fig harvest with a frenzied ritual of copulation. Cherries are designed to please, especially if you're feeding each other, while bananas are believed to contain an enzyme that enhances the male sexual function.

Whether you believe in aphrodisiacs or not, the way you eat food can be as erotic and sensual as the food itself. The sight of raw oyster flesh quivering in its shell is enough to make your endorphins rise. Feeding an elegant asparagus spear to your loved one and watching the butter drip down their chin can be just as sexy as eating the tender tips yourself. Or how about sharing a tub of ice cream *in* the tub, steamy suds contrasting with ice-cold spoonfuls of your favourite flavour as the spoon is passed from mouth to mouth? A heady combination indeed. Gordon Ramsay advocates the icy texture as a phenomenal sensuous success: 'You just want to sit opposite your partner, ask them to close their eyes and drop a very nice dollop of peach sorbet in their mouth, followed by a sip of pink champagne. That's quite mind-blowing, very sexy. You could have that in bed quite easily.'

Just the process of preparing food for someone special shows a great deal of love and affection. Ainsley Harriot believes that if you're passionate about someone, it doesn't matter what you eat: 'I can get turned on eating an orange with my wife. Food is an incredibly sensual thing. There are ways of sending messages: touching the bread roll at the same time, finding yourself picking up the drink at the same time so you're looking over the glass at each other. Of course they're sensual, and I think that food is the second thing to sex, if you like.'

In the Cornish village of Padstow, Elizabeth and Peter Prideaux-Brune indulge in their own special dish of love every year for their wedding anniversary breakfast. Just the name 'Oeufs à l'Amour' ('Eggs of Love') conjures up romance, and the important thing is that they prepare the dish together:

Oeufs à l'Amour   Serves 2

Gently scrambled eggs are lifted to new heights in this dish, returned to their shells with caviar.

- 2 large fresh eggs
- 25 g (1 oz) unsalted butter
- salt and freshly ground pepper
- 2 small blobs of thick double cream, crème fraîche or sour cream
- 1 tablespoon caviar
- small pieces of toast, cut into heart shapes, to garnish

1. Using a sharp knife, take the top off each egg, working over a plate to catch the white as it runs out. Empty the eggs into a bowl. Wash the shells – bottoms and lids – carefully in warm water. Set them aside on paper towels to dry. If necessary, trim the shells for presentation.

2. With a fork, lightly beat the eggs. Scramble the eggs with the butter: cook them very slowly in a buttered bain-marie, with the butter cut into tiny cubes, add some salt and pepper and stir more or less continuously with a wooden spoon, until the mixture is very soft and creamy.

3. Fill the two bottom shells with the scrambled egg mixture. Add a tiny blob of cream to each, then top with caviar. Finally, pop on the lids, so as to resemble little hats. Garnish with small pieces of heart-shaped toast.

We want to give pleasure and satisfaction, and food will do just that if it's delivered in the right way. A bottle of champagne to break the ice; candles sending flickering shadows around the room; music playing softly in the background: all help to create the right ambience. Sadly, a quarter of the population of Britain don't have their own favourite food of love. Perhaps these recipes will inspire them . . .

1

Strawberries and Cream

One in five chose this dish as the most romantic, and the vote was almost equally split between men and women. A staggering 40 per cent of people in Northern Ireland voted strawberries and cream the top turn-on.

It's worth waiting for British strawberries to hit the supermarket shelves as their taste is often far superior to that of their imported counterparts. If you're out to impress a new date, try this seriously sexy combination of strawberry, meringue and passion fruit.

Passionate Strawberry Crush

- 450 g (1 lb) fresh strawberries, stalks removed
- 4 tablespoons icing sugar
- 200 ml (7 fl oz) double cream
- 2 passion fruit, halved (to ensure they're ripe, buy the wrinkled ones)
- 6 tablespoons Greek yoghurt
- 4 soft meringue nests, bought or home-made, crushed into pieces

1. Remove the hulls from the strawberries and roughly chop half of the fruit. Tip into a small saucepan with 2 tablespoons of the icing sugar and place the pan over a gentle heat. Cook for about 1 minute until the strawberries are softening. Pour into a sieve over a bowl and push through all the juices using the back of a ladle, leaving behind any seeds. Taste for sweetness, adding extra icing sugar if necessary. Leave to cool and chill in the fridge.

2. Whisk together the double cream and remaining icing sugar until it forms soft peaks. Lightly mash the remaining strawberries with the back of a fork and gently stir into the cream with the passion fruit flesh, Greek yoghurt and crushed meringue. Spoon into a large serving bowl and pour over the strawberry sauce. This delectable bowl of passion can be made at least 2 hours in advance and kept cool or in the fridge until you feel the moment is right.

STRAWBERRY CRISPS
As a delicious addition to the finished strawberry crush, make these wonderfully intense strawberry crisps to sprinkle over the top just before serving.

- 250 g (9 oz) strawberries, stalks removed

1. Pre-heat the oven to 110°C/225°F/Gas Mark $^1/_4$.

2. Slice the strawberries very thinly. Blot any excess juices with kitchen paper and lay on a baking tray lined with silicone paper. Place in the oven for 1 hour until becoming dry, turn over, then continue to dry out in the oven until crisp but not golden. This could take up to a further 1–1$^1/_2$ hours. Turn off the oven and leave to cool. If you are not using the crisps straight away, store them in an airtight container.

2

Chocolate

Chocolate is arguably the greatest food of love, believed to have qualities that increase sexual appetite. According to our survey, the younger you are, the more likely you are to choose chocolate for seduction, while nearly a third of those in Wales said it was their favourite.

Apparently, chocolate was Casanova's preferred bedtime drink, believed to give him the stamina of a stallion. The Aztec king Montezuma claimed it made him more virile, and they even banned chocolate from monasteries a few centuries ago. Valentine's Day wouldn't be complete without gifts of chocolate, and they play a big part in the wooing process. Try making this sophisticated cake in advance of your date and wait for the effects to start ...

Chocolate Heart Cake with Chocolate Glaze

- 300 g (11 oz) good-quality dark chocolate (at least 70 per cent cocoa solids), broken into pieces
- 250 g (9 oz) unsalted butter
- 5 eggs, separated
- 1–2 tablespoons brandy, amaretto or Grand Marnier
- 75 g (3 oz) caster sugar
- 100 g (4 oz) self-raising flour
- pinch of salt

GLAZE
- 175 g (6 oz) good-quality dark chocolate, broken into pieces
- 200 ml (7 fl oz) double cream

20 cm (8 in) heart-shaped cake tin, greased and lined with baking paper. If you can't get a heart-shaped tin, use a round tin and cut the cake into a heart shape when cooked.

1. Pre-heat the oven to 150°C/300°F/Gas Mark 2.

2. To make the cake, place the chocolate and butter in a bowl over a pan of gently simmering water. Leave until melted and smooth, stirring only once or twice. Allow to cool slightly. Keep the pan of water to use for making the glaze, as anything that saves on the washing up is always a bonus!

3. Place the egg yolks, brandy or liqueur and sugar in a bowl and whisk until thickened and creamy, ideally with an electric whisk. Fold in the cooled chocolate mixture, then sift the flour over the top, also folding in until all of the flour is incorporated.

4. Whisk the egg whites with the salt until they form soft peaks. Gently fold into the chocolate mixture until completely combined, being careful not to knock out all of the air. Pour the mixture into the heart-shaped tin and bake for 50 minutes–1 hour or until just firm to the touch. Remove from the oven and allow to cool in the tin.

5. While the cake is cooking, make the rich, gooey glaze. Put the chocolate and cream in a bowl and place over the pan of gently simmering water (the one you saved from making the cake). Leave without stirring until the chocolate has just melted, then briefly stir until smooth. This can now be left to cool at room temperature until it reaches a soft, spreadable consistency.

6. Turn the cake out of the tin on to a large serving plate. Lightly spread the glaze over the top of the cake, creating a heart-shaped swirl in the centre. Now all you need is your other half and a couple of forks.

3

Asparagus

The French have a reputation as great romantics, and the aphrodisiac qualities of this delicious vegetable were part of the wedding ritual in 19th-century France. It was decreed that bridegrooms should be served three courses of asparagus at their prenuptial dinner in preparation for the long night ahead. Asparagus apparently helps to alleviate stress, so this is an ideal starter for that nervous first date.

Naughty Nibble (Tender Asparagus in Melted Lemon and Parmesan Butter)   Serves 2

- 2 generous tablespoons butter, at room temperature
- grated zest of $\frac{1}{2}$ small lemon
- 2 tablespoons finely grated Parmesan cheese
- garlic salt
- 12–16 asparagus spears
- flaked sea salt

1. Mix together the butter, lemon zest and grated Parmesan and season with garlic salt (don't worry about the garlic – if you're both eating it, you won't notice!). Put to one side.

2. Snap the asparagus 2–4 cm ($\frac{3}{4}$–1$\frac{1}{2}$ in) from the base of the stalks. The spears should naturally find their own breaking point. If the asparagus is particularly thick, trim away any tough-looking pointy ears on the stalk, as these can have a bitter taste.

3. Place the asparagus in a wide saucepan or large, deep frying pan of rapidly boiling salted water. Cook for 2–4 minutes (depending on their thickness) until just tender. Remove from the water with a slotted spoon and shake off any excess water. Place on a warm plate and sit the flavoured butter on top. Turn the asparagus so the butter is melting and oozing over every spear, then sprinkle over some sea salt.
Now all you need to do is feed each other the asparagus, with the melted butter dribbling down your chin and your fingers.

TIP
If your time together is too precious to be spent cooking asparagus, you can do it in advance:

Slightly undercook the asparagus in the boiling water, remove with a slotted spoon and instantly drop into iced water for a few seconds to stop the cooking process. Lift out, shake off any excess water and keep covered in the fridge. When you are ready, the asparagus can be heated up in a microwave or briefly dropped into boiling water until hot, and then served with the butter.

4

Smoked Salmon

According to our survey, if you were born between 1948 and 1957 you're more likely to choose smoked salmon to impress your loved one. Once a rare treat for special occasions, smoked salmon is now widely available at a reasonable price. Look for smoked Scottish salmon instead of Scottish smoked salmon (which just means it's any old salmon that's been smoked in Scotland) if you want the best flavour.

Seductive Salmon   Serves 2

- 12 thin slices of rye or pumpernickel bread
- 4 tablespoons cream cheese
- 1 teaspoon capers, drained and chopped
- 1 teaspoon hot horseradish sauce
- 1 lemon
- salt and freshly ground black pepper
- 125 g (4 $\frac{1}{2}$ oz) pack of sliced smoked salmon

1. Using a heart-shaped cutter approximately 5–6 cm (2–2 $\frac{1}{2}$ in) in diameter, cut out hearts from the slices of bread. If you can't get hold of rye or pumpernickel bread, you can use mini blinis or lightly toasted, thinly sliced brown bread.

2. Place the cream cheese, capers and horseradish in a small bowl. Finely grate in a little lemon zest – the amount you add is up to you, depending on how tart you're feeling! Cut the lemon in half and add a small squeeze of the juice. Season with salt and pepper and mix together.

3. Spread or pipe the cream cheese mixture on to the centre of the heart-shaped bread. Place twists of smoked salmon on top and arrange on a plate. For the perfect partnership, serve with an ice-cold shot of lemon-flavoured vodka.

5 Prawns

Prawns are the perfect finger food and can be peeled lovingly for your partner. People in England are twice as likely to eat prawns on a big date than those in Scotland, Wales and Northern Ireland.

This recipe calls for champagne to marinate the prawns and to add to the batter, so buy a big bottle (a magnum) if you want to glug while you're peeling, and get your partner to help out.

Champagne Prawns with Cocktail Sauce   Serves 2

- 16 large raw prawns, shelled, with tails attached
- 150–175 ml (5–6 fl oz) chilled champagne or sparkling wine
- oil, for deep frying
- 100 g (4 oz) self-raising flour, plus 2 tablespoons for dusting
- salt and freshly ground black pepper
- lemon wedges, to serve

COCKTAIL SAUCE
- 3 heaped tablespoons mayonnaise
- 1 tablespoon tomato ketchup
- 1 teaspoon Worcestershire sauce
- few drops of Tabasco sauce
- few drops of soy sauce
- squeeze of lemon juice
- celery salt and freshly ground black pepper

1. First of all, make the cocktail sauce. This is best done with your partner – although it may take twice as long! One of you drops the mayonnaise, ketchup, Worcestershire sauce, Tabasco, soy and lemon juice into a bowl while the other mixes to a smooth consistency. Season with celery salt and pepper. Have a taste and add any extras if you both agree on it, then transfer to a small bowl and put to one side while you prepare the prawns.

2. If you've bought the prawns with the head and shell attached, prepare them between you – this is real teamwork, and although it may not be sensual, it will take half the time. Place the prepared prawns with about 2–3 tablespoons of the champagne or sparkling wine in a non-metallic bowl to marinate for about 30 minutes.

3. Place enough oil in a wok, large saucepan or deep-fat fryer to come halfway up the pan. Place over a medium heat. If you're using a deep-fat fryer or have a thermometer, heat the oil to 180°C/350°F. If not, check the oil is at the right temperature by dropping a 2–3 cm (³/₄–1¹/₄ in) cube of bread into it. It should become golden and crispy in 1 minute.

4. Sift the flour and a generous pinch of salt into a large bowl. Whisk in enough of the champagne or sparkling wine to give a thick batter. Add the remaining liquid if it seems too gluey. The best way to do this is if one of you pours while the other whisks.

5. Remove the prawns from the marinade and pat dry with kitchen paper. Season with salt and pepper and lightly toss in the 2 tablespoons of flour. Holding the tail, dip each prawn into the batter to coat and place into the hot oil. Keep hold of the tail for a couple of seconds before letting go. This will stop them sticking to each other or the base of the pan. Continue with the remaining prawns. Allow them to cook for about 6–7 minutes until golden and crispy, turning in the oil halfway through to ensure even cooking.

6. Once they are cooked, carefully remove the battered prawns from the oil and sit on kitchen paper to allow any excess oil to drain away. Sprinkle with salt and serve on one plate to share with the cocktail sauce and lemon wedges.

6

Oysters/Mussels

Oysters have long been considered one of the most erotic foods, perhaps more because of their appearance than of any discernible aphrodisiac effects. Mussels were equally popular with our voters, and are probably less of a challenge to eat than oysters, which many consider an acquired taste. You can use either mussels or oysters in these saucy ideas.

Saucy Seafood

These three luscious sauces are perfect spooned over as many mussels or oysters as you want.

TO COOK THE MUSSELS
You can buy cooked mussels from fish counters; however, they're far better if you cook them yourself. For this recipe try to buy New Zealand green-lipped mussels as they're large and meaty when cooked.

1. Wash well under cold running water and remove any stringy beards by pulling sharply. Throw out any mussels that have damaged or open shells.

2. Heat a glassful of water in a large saucepan over a high heat. Once the water is boiling, drop in the mussels, shake around and cover with a lid. Leave to steam for 3–5 minutes, or until the shells have opened, shaking the pan a couple of times.

3. Tip into a colander and throw out any mussels that haven't opened. Remove the empty top shells of each one and gently loosen the mussel in the other half. These can now be served warm straight away or left to cool and placed on a platter of crushed ice. Eat with one or all of the sauces opposite.

TO OPEN THE OYSTERS
This isn't the easiest job in the world, but with a bit of practice you'll soon be an expert; or simply ask your fishmonger to do it for you.

1. Hold the oyster flat-side upwards with a cloth or tea towel over a bowl to catch waste shells and any mess. You'll need a small table knife or oyster shuck, though the job is actually easier using a clean screwdriver. Whichever tool you are using, insert it into the pointed tip of the oyster. Push and twist around to prise open the shell; be patient as some are easier than others. Remove the empty shell and gently loosen the oyster in the other half.

2. Place on a platter of crushed ice and enjoy slurping straight away with one or all of the following sauces.

SAUCE 1:
ORIENTAL PLEASURE

- $\frac{1}{2}$ red chilli, finely chopped
- 2 tablespoons rice wine vinegar or white wine vinegar
- 1 small clove of garlic, crushed
- 2 teaspoons caster sugar
- 1 teaspoon grated fresh ginger
- about 1 tablespoon chopped coriander leaves

Mix together all of the ingredients, leave for about 30 minutes to allow the flavours to infuse, then serve in a small bowl to spoon over the oysters.

SAUCE 2:
HOT STUFF

- a few good shakes of Tabasco sauce
- juice of $\frac{1}{2}$ lemon
- twist of freshly ground black pepper

Mix all of the ingredients together and drizzle sparingly over the opened oysters.

SAUCE 3:
GETTING FRESH

- $\frac{1}{4}$ cucumber
- good squeeze of lime juice
- 1 teaspoon roughly chopped fresh dill or chervil
- pinch of caster sugar

Quarter the cucumber lengthways and remove the seeds. Cut the flesh into thin matchsticks and mix together with the lime juice and dill or chervil. Leave for about 30 minutes to allow the flavours to develop, then serve in a small bowl to spoon over the oysters.

7 Chocolate Mousse

These sumptuous white chocolate mousses are served with a layer of warm espresso coffee and coffee liqueur on top. As both the chocolate and coffee have aphrodisiac qualities, you'll have double the fun.

Double Delight   Makes 2–4, depending on the size of coffee cups used

- 100 g (4 oz) white chocolate, broken into pieces (Milky Bar is ideal as it has a really creamy taste)
- 2 tablespoons cold water
- 150 ml (5 fl oz) double cream
- 1 egg white
- 1 warm shot of espresso mixed with a good glug of coffee liqueur, to serve

1. Place the chocolate and water in a bowl over a pan of gently simmering water and leave to melt slowly. Remove from the heat, stir and leave to cool for about 5 minutes.

2. Whip the cream until it thickens to form soft peaks and, in a separate bowl, whisk the egg white until it also forms soft peaks.

3. Pour the melted chocolate into the whipped cream and gently stir in. Fold in the egg white before spooning into coffee cups, making sure you leave about 1 cm (1/2 in) of a rim at the top for the coffee.

4. Place in the fridge for about 2–3 hours until set. Just before serving, pour over the warm espresso and coffee liqueur mixture and enjoy straight away.

8 Strawberries Dipped in Chocolate

This is the only dish in the top ten over which men and women differed in their choice of sexy food. Nearly twice as many women voted this their favourite, with Scotland and Northern Ireland topping the dipping charts. For this dish you'll have great fun flirting over the fondue and fishing out the fruits with your fingers.

Flirtatious Fondue with Strawberries

- 150 g (5 oz) plain chocolate, such as Bournville, broken into pieces
- 200 ml (7 fl oz) double cream
- 15 g (1/2 oz) butter
- 1–2 tablespoons Cointreau or Grand Marnier
- 1 large punnet of lush, ripe strawberries, long-stemmed if possible

1. Place the chocolate, cream, butter and Cointreau or Grand Marnier in a bowl over a pan of gently simmering water and leave until the chocolate and butter have melted. Stir until mixed together and transfer to a small fondue bowl over a lit fondue heater.

2. Wash the strawberries and pat dry. Holding on to the stalks, dip them into the fondue.

TIP
Any leftover chocolate sauce needn't be wasted – you can have plenty of fun using it as a body paint, providing it's not too hot.

9 Champagne and Caviar

Champagne inspires feelings of celebration, indulgence, luxury and lust. Just popping the cork signals a night of passion, and when the bubbles start to go to the head it's time to get out the caviar and let the high zinc content work its magic (apparently zinc increases the promotion of testosterone and caviar eggs popping on the tongue stimulate sexual desire). This indulgent treat is a favourite with all age groups, but is six times more popular in London than in Northern Ireland.

Cupid's Caviar Serves 2 for nibbling

- 10–12 baby new potatoes
- 1 small Granny Smith apple, peeled, cored and grated
- 4 tablespoons crème fraîche
- squeeze of lemon juice
- salt and freshly ground black pepper
- 30 g (1¼ oz) tin of caviar (see tips, right)
- a few chive stalks, cut into 5 mm (¼ in) pieces

1. Cook the potatoes in boiling salted water until tender. This will take about 10–12 minutes. Drain, then leave in the saucepan, covered with a tea towel, for 5 minutes. This will give a fluffier texture to the potatoes. Cut each one in half and slice a thin slither off the skin end so they sit flat on a serving plate, cut-side up. These can now be left to cool completely.

2. Firmly squeeze all excess liquid from the apple into a glass – you will be surprised how much liquid comes out – and you now have a really fresh glass of apple juice to drink. Mix the grated apple with the crème fraîche and lemon juice and season with salt and pepper. Spoon a little on top of each cooled potato half, then carefully place a small spoonful of caviar on top. To finish, add a twist of pepper and a couple of chive stalks.

SOME USEFUL TIPS WHEN BUYING CAVIAR
Beluga caviar is sold in a blue tin and is the most highly regarded and expensive. It is large-grained and grey or (rarely) golden in colour. Oscietreis caviar is sold in a yellow can. It is medium-grained and varies in colour from golden brown/bottle green/grey to bluish white. Sevruga caviar is sold in a red tin and is less expensive. It is small-grained and greeny black in colour.

Bellini Cocktail Makes 4 glasses for 2 people – 1 each simply won't be enough

This famous luxurious cocktail was invented at Harry's Bar, Venice, in 1934 and is the perfect accompaniment to the Cupid's Caviar.

- 2 ripe peaches, peeled, halved and stone removed, or the equivalent using tinned peaches in natural juice
- chilled champagne or sparkling wine
- 2 chilled champagne glasses

1. Place the peaches in a small blender and purée until totally smooth. This can be done well in advance and kept in the fridge. Spoon half into the chilled champagne glasses and slowly top up with champagne, stirring as you pour. You should ideally have one third peach purée to two thirds champagne. Serve straight away as a pre-dinner drink with the Cupid's Caviar, leaving plenty of time for a second glass each.

10   Ice Cream

The food of love for the younger generation, with under-25s four times more likely to turn to the ice-cream tub than the over-55s. It's so easy to buy really good ice cream from the supermarket, but wouldn't it be impressive to serve up an indulgent creamy toffee and marshmallow ice of your own?

Indulgent Iced Bliss
Makes plenty for 2 if you're feeling greedy or self-indulgent – but beware, it's very rich

- 150 g (5 oz) bought soft toffees
- 150 ml (5 fl oz) full-fat milk
- 150 ml (5 fl oz) double cream
- 100 ml (3¹/₂ fl oz) crème fraîche
- couple of large handfuls of mini marshmallows (or normal-sized ones cut up with scissors)

1. Place 50 g (2 oz) of the toffees in a plastic sandwich bag and put in the freezer. Place the remaining toffees in a saucepan with the milk and stir over a gentle heat until the toffees have dissolved. Remove from the heat and leave until completely cool, stirring occasionally.

2. Whip the double cream until it forms soft peaks, then stir in the crème fraîche and toffee milk. Pour into an ice-cream machine and churn until it is beginning to thicken.

3. Remove the toffees from the freezer and bash into small chunks with a rolling pin. Add the marshmallows and chopped toffees to the ice-cream machine and continue to churn until the ice cream is thick and scoopable. Ideally eat straight away out of the container while it's at this perfect consistency, with a long Knickerbocker Glory spoon shared between the two of you.

TIPS
If you're making the ice cream in advance, transfer to the freezer in a covered container (it will keep for up to 3 weeks), then transfer to the fridge 30 minutes before eating.
If you don't have an ice-cream machine, place the mixture in a container (preferably metal) and freeze, beating well at hourly intervals, adding the marshmallows and toffee when it's thickening.

Try using other flavours instead of the marshmallows, such as pecan or pistachio nuts, chocolate chunks, Maltesers, chunks of a Crunchie bar or broken ginger snap biscuits.

5:
Nation's Favourite
Convenience Food

Churchill called fish and chips 'the good companions' and most people wouldn't consider having one without the other. It's one of the few dishes we'd eat straight from the paper and it's perfectly acceptable to enjoy eating it on the street. Let's wave the proverbial flag for fish and chips and celebrate this marriage made in heaven as Britain's first choice for convenience food.

Aside from London and Scotland, every other area of the nation voted for fish and chips as their favourite take-away or ready meal. The French introduced us to *pommes frites* (fried potatoes) in 1865 and we've been revelling in chips ever since. By 1927 there were 35,000 fish and chip shops in Britain, but that number's fallen to a mere 9,000 today. Nevertheless, we still eat 22,000 tons of chips a week.

It's interesting to note that fish and chips are the only traditional British dish to appear in the top ten. Chinese, Indian, Thai and Italian cuisine form the rest of the favourites. Convenience foods have been with us for years and yet it's only recently we've recognized them as such. Fray Bentos steak and kidney pies and Vesta curries were early versions of the convenient meal. We can open a tin, tear a packet open or defrost something from the freezer, and now we can buy prepared sauces, part-baked breads, chilled pastry and the like. Our weekday meals have become quick, easy and versatile.

We eat something like 70 million Indian and 110 million Chinese meals a year, and yet our version of Chinese food in this country bears little resemblance to traditional Chinese dishes. Chow mein won't be found anywhere on a menu in China, yet it's the sixth most popular convenience food here. When Nigel Slater was asked what chow mein meant to him, he admitted he didn't know what the dish was: 'It doesn't really matter what it is because if you chose that you'd probably be too pissed to notice.' Ainsley Harriott agrees: 'Chow mein is one of those things that nobody knows what it is. It's kind of "Let's use everything up, here they come. They've had 15 pints of lager, just throw everything in the silver box" and then they scribble something on the top which makes it look authentic.'

Chicken tikka masala previously held the title as Britain's favourite dish, but in our survey it's been relegated to number four. Food writer Madhur Jaffrey questions the authenticity of this popular dish. 'Chicken tikka masala is of Indian origin, but its present form is very British. First you make a tandoori chicken tikka, so you have small pieces of meat that have been marinated and then grilled in a tandoor. The traditional way would be to serve it as is or to make a butter tomato sauce. Then somebody in England decided to make a very quick curry-type sauce and throw the chicken tikka in it, and that became the chicken tikka masala of England.'

Fast food is quick and cheap but we don't always know what take-aways contain. It's possible to make similar food at home in a convenient way, safe in the knowledge that there are no hidden ingredients.

1

Fish and Chips

A fifth of the population voted for fish and chips as a quick and easy meal. Once you've made fish and chips at home you'll find it hard to go back to the bought ones. It's worth using a deep-fat fryer for both safety and convenience. If you don't have one, make sure you have a kitchen thermometer to check the oil is at the right temperature. Using lager in the batter gives a wonderful flavour and light texture.

Deep-fried Fish in Beer Batter and Chips

- beef dripping or oil, for deep frying (beef dripping is used in the traditional method and gives a far better flavour, but sunflower or vegetable oil will work just as well)

FISH
- 4 x 175 g (6 oz) thick cod or haddock fillets, taken from the head end rather than the tail end of the fish
- 225 g (8 oz) self-raising flour, plus extra for dusting
- salt and freshly ground black pepper
- 300 ml (10 fl oz) fridge-cold lager

CHIPS
- 6–8 large floury potatoes, such as Maris Piper, King Edward, Desiree (depending on how hungry you are)

1. Pre-heat the oven to 150°C/300°F/Gas Mark 2 and pre-heat the dripping or oil to 120°C/250°F.

2. For the chips, peel the potatoes and cut into whatever size you prefer. Wash well in cold water, drain and pat dry with a clean tea towel. Put the potatoes into the fryer and allow them to fry gently for about 8–10 minutes, until they are soft but still pale. Check they're cooked by piercing with a small, sharp knife. Lift out of the pan and leave to cool slightly on greaseproof paper.

3. Increase the heat of the fryer to 180°C/350°F.

4. Season the fish and dust lightly with flour; this enables the batter to stick to the fish.

5. To make the batter, sift the flour and a pinch of salt into a large bowl and whisk in the lager to give a thick batter, adding a little extra beer if it seems over-thick. It should be the consistency of very thick double cream and should coat the back of a wooden spoon. Season with salt and thickly coat 2 of the fillets with the batter. Carefully place in the hot fat and cook for 8–10 minutes until golden and crispy. Remove from the pan, drain and sit on a baking sheet lined with greaseproof paper, then keep warm in the oven while you cook the remaining 2 fillets in the same way.

6. Once the fish is cooked, return the chips to the fryer and cook for 2–3 minutes or until golden and crispy. Shake off any excess fat and season with salt before serving with the crispy fish and Quick Tartare Sauce. If liked, you can serve with tinned mushy peas and bread and butter, for the authentic experience!

Quick Tartare Sauce

- 200 ml (7 fl oz) mayonnaise
- 3 tablespoons capers, drained and chopped
- 3 tablespoons gherkins, drained and chopped
- 1 small shallot, finely chopped
- squeeze of lemon juice
- 3 tablespoons chopped fresh parsley
- flaked sea salt and freshly ground black pepper

Mix together all of the ingredients in a small bowl and serve straight away or store in the fridge until needed.

2

Pizza

Although pizza came second in our survey, 28 per cent of vegetarians voted it their favourite convenience food, making it number one for non-meat eaters. Traditional Italian pizza combines a good tomato sauce with some first-class mozzarella cheese and a sprinkling of herbs, but you can add a whole variety of ingredients. Here's an easy recipe for a pizza base with a basic tomato sauce: the choice of topping is yours.

Quick Home-made Pizza   Makes 1 large (approx. 30 cm/12 in) or 2 small (approx. 23 cm/9 in) pizzas

BASE
- 1 double packet of pizza dough mix (2 x 145 g sachets)
- add any of these suggestions to flavour the dough: 1 teaspoon dried chilli flakes, a small handful of finely grated Parmesan cheese, 1 teaspoon dried or 1 tablespoon chopped fresh herbs (oregano, basil, parsley, thyme, marjoram, rosemary), 1–2 tablespoons finely chopped sun-dried tomatoes, 1–2 tablespoons finely chopped olives, 1 tablespoon flavoured oil, such as chilli, basil or rosemary
- flour, for rolling out
- olive oil, for drizzling

TOMATO SAUCE
- 2 tablespoons olive oil
- 1 medium onion, finely chopped
- 2 cloves of garlic, crushed
- 1 bay leaf
- 1 teaspoon dried oregano
- 400 g (14 oz) tin of chopped tomatoes
- 2 tablespoons tomato purée
- flaked sea salt and freshly ground black pepper

1. Make the base according to the packet instructions, using both packets to make a double amount of dough. It can be left plain, but for a more interesting pizza add your chosen flavouring from the suggestions (left) before any liquid is added.

2. Roll into 1 large pizza base or 2 smaller ones, sit on a baking sheet(s) and leave to rise in a warm place. While the dough is rising you can prepare the tomato sauce and toppings.

3. For the sauce, heat the olive oil in a medium saucepan and gently cook the onion and garlic for about 8 minutes until softened. Add the remaining ingredients and simmer for 10 minutes until you have a thick, spreadable sauce. Season with salt and pepper, then remove the bay leaf.

4. Pre-heat the oven to 220°C/425°F/Gas Mark 7.

5. Spread a generous amount of tomato sauce over the pizza base(s), leaving a 1 cm ($1/2$ in) gap around the edge. You can now add your favourite toppings (see overleaf for some suggestions), drizzle with olive oil, then place in the oven for about 15–20 minutes or until the base is crisp and the topping is golden.

(CONTINUED OVERLEAF)

2 continued

Topping Suggestions

Tomato and cheese form the basic pizza ingredients, but depending on your mood and your taste buds, you can turn a basic pizza into any flavour you like. Experiment yourself or try some of these suggestions:

CHEESE FEAST
- 120 g (4 ½ oz) each of mozzarella, Gruyère, Dolcelatte and 50 g (2 oz) Parmesan cheese

POPEYE SPECIAL
- 50 g (2 oz) cooked spinach, grated nutmeg, 1 teaspoon dried oregano, 50 g (2 oz) mozzarella cheese, a handful of grated Parmesan cheese, a handful of pinenuts and 1 egg broken in the centre

HOT HOT HOT
- thinly sliced pepperoni, thinly sliced onion, a few chopped jalapeño peppers, mozzarella cheese and oregano

FOUR-IN-ONE
- place thinly sliced pepperoni/salami over one quarter of the top, thinly sliced mushrooms over the second quarter, mozzarella cheese over the third quarter and tinned anchovies, olives and capers over the last quarter

PIZZA MED
- a few slices of Parma ham, mozzarella cheese, sun-dried tomatoes, basil, olives and Parmesan cheese

SEAFOOD AND SPICE
- cooked prawns, capers, olives, chilli flakes, mozzarella cheese and tinned anchovies

6:
Nation's Favourite
Outdoor Food

Vying for top position in the category of outdoor food (including picnics, packed lunches and barbecues) are two popular components of the British diet. The winner comes from the picnic and packed-lunch category and forms a major part of most people's culinary lives. So let's celebrate the success of the sandwich – one of the easiest foods to consume outside and the main feature of many a school lunchbox or pastoral picnic.

Many people say that food tastes better when eaten outside. Is this true, or is it just that, unlike our Mediterranean neighbours, we so seldom get the opportunity to dine *al fresco* in this country? Whatever you believe, it appears that as a nation we enjoy the pleasures of outdoor dining – from a hamper at Glyndebourne to a picnic on the beach or a barbecue in the back garden.

We've all experienced it – even though the man of the house never normally enters the kitchen, he automatically takes charge of the barbecue. Rick Stein has a theory about this: 'It's to do with being in the scouts and building camp fires, it's a sort of hunting instinct, and there's something very primeval about cooking a piece

of meat outdoors. But most men do it so badly.' In fact, it's very easy to barbecue food badly. The flames are often too high, burning the meat on the outside and leaving it raw in the middle. It may seem like an easy way to cook but you must be prepared for all kinds of hazards. A successful barbecue requires careful preparation, good raw ingredients and, above all, perfectly glowing coals.

The barbecue has recently become a major feature of most people's summer gardens, but the picnic dates back some 400 years and the British have always excelled in this extraordinary ritual. It started as a feast for hunters when portable foods such as pastries, pies and hams allowed the hunting to continue without the interruption of returning to the house for a meal. A perfect picnic food is pork pie, as it's ready packaged in a crisp pastry that's unlikely to crumble during transportation. Sadly, this didn't appear in the top ten, but 24 per cent of the population still voted pork pie into 15th place, just behind quiche at number 14.

Transporting food to a picnic can often be tricky. Hampers look the part and often come ready stacked with matching plates, cups, glasses, flasks and napkins. But the invention of the cool-box has rendered the hamper pretty useless, unless you're out to impress. The most important rule of all is to make dishes that are hard-wearing and keep salad dressings separate until you're ready to eat. Pasta or potato salads, whole roast chickens, quiches and pasties can all be prepared in advance and make an impressive display on a picnic rug or tablecloth. Consider Gary Rhodes' advice for dessert: 'Forget making the cheesecake as it'll only get squashed and the blackcurrant topping will fall off the side. Why don't you just have some English strawberries with a little pot of cream? Is there a better dessert on a summer's day?'

1

Sandwiches

The sandwich is an everyday favourite with 40 per cent of the nation. But in Scotland and Northern Ireland over half the population said they preferred a sandwich for a picnic or packed lunch.

You want to avoid soggy cheese and tomato sandwiches on a picnic, so this stuffed baguette is a perfect solution. You can make it well in advance and it will feed lots of people.

Stuffed Baguette

1. Buy a baguette as big as you require and slice it in half lengthways. Scoop out the bread from the top and bottom halves. This can be blitzed to breadcrumbs and used in other recipes, or fed to the birds.

2. In the hollow base of the baguette, layer up very generously with whatever fillings you fancy (try some of the suggestions below), seasoning with a dressing of your choice or just salt and pepper as you go. Once you've filled enough to resemble the shape of the original baguette, place the top half of the stick back on. Wrap tightly in cling film and leave for a few hours in the fridge.

3. When ready to eat, unwrap and slice into individual chunks, allowing them to reach room temperature to enhance the flavours before eating.

Suggested Fillings

These are ideal fillings for the above, or for tortilla wraps, bread rolls, pitta bread or ciabatta. If you're using ordinary sliced bread, be careful not to make the fillings too wet as the bread will soak up the juices and turn into a floppy mess.

- tuna with chopped olives, capers, red onion, parsley, lemon juice and olive oil
- crab meat (fresh or tinned) with spring onion, sweetcorn, fresh coriander, sweet chilli sauce and soy sauce
- avocado, Parma ham, toasted pinenuts, sun-dried tomatoes, Parmesan cheese, rocket

- cooked shelled prawns with cucumber and dill mayonnaise
- sliced cooked meats or ham with salad and chutney or mustard
- sliced Swiss cheese, chargrilled peppers, tomatoes, salad leaves and mayonnaise
- hummus with grilled or marinated peppers or aubergines, mint and rocket

6

Chicken Wings/Drumsticks

For some, a barbecue is not complete without the obligatory chicken wings and drumsticks, yet they came only sixth in our survey. Enjoyed by all age groups in all areas of the country, they're ideal for both a barbecue and a picnic box. If you're barbecuing them, cook them first so people have something to munch with a drink while they're waiting for the main attraction.

Oriental Sticky Chicken Wings/Drumsticks   Makes 12

- 6 chicken drumsticks, preferably free-range
- 6 chicken wings, preferably free-range

MARINADE
- 2 tablespoons runny honey
- 3 cm (1¼ in) piece of fresh ginger, peeled and grated
- 1 clove of garlic, crushed
- 1½ teaspoons Chinese five spice
- 2 teaspoons soy sauce
- 3 tablespoons orange marmalade
- ½ teaspoon grated orange zest
- 1 tablespoon sesame seeds
- 1 tablespoon sesame oil

1. Slash the chicken drumsticks 3–4 times each with a sharp knife and place in a non-metallic bowl with the chicken wings. Mix together all of the marinade ingredients and pour over the chicken. Leave to marinate for at least 2 hours, or overnight if you can, turning occasionally.

2. Once it has marinated, place the chicken on the barbecue over medium-hot coals and cook for about 20 minutes, brushing with any marinade left in the dish as it cooks. If it's colouring too quickly, move to a cooler part of the barbecue to cook more gently. It's important you cook the chicken all the way through. If you're unsure, pierce a drumstick with a skewer: if the juices are still pink, carry on cooking. Eat as soon as they're cool enough to handle, with the sticky sauce all around your mouth and fingers. Isn't that what barbecues are all about?

OVEN COOKING
The chicken can also be cooked in the oven for perfect picnic food:

1. Pre-heat the oven to 200°C/400°F/Gas Mark 6.

2. Transfer the chicken into a roasting tray with a couple of spoonfuls of marinade. Place in the oven for about 50 minutes, turning occasionally and basting with the marinade/juices until thoroughly sticky and golden, adding extra marinade to the tray if necessary. Once the chicken pieces are cooked, eat them when fresh and hot, or leave to cool before packing up for a picnic or packed lunch.

7

Bread and Cheese

The French know the importance of good bread and cheese, but the British can also enjoy the delights of this simple yet delicious combination. British cheeses are some of the finest in the world and the regional specialities are definitely worth considering as an addition to your picnic basket. If you can track them down, try Beenleigh Blue from Totnes in Devon, Cornish Yarg from Liskeard, Cheddar from Somerset, Wensleydale from North Yorkshire or Caerphilly from Wales. If you take the cheeses straight from the fridge for a picnic, they'll be at just the right temperature for eating by the time you reach your destination.

It's better to take bread in a complete loaf to prevent it drying out, so a whole baguette or some crusty fresh ciabatta rolls are ideal. Whatever bread and cheese you choose, this chutney is a perfect accompaniment.

Apple, Date and Ginger Chutney
Makes approx. 1.5 litres (2½ pints)

- 1.5 kg (3 lb) Bramley apples
- 2 cloves of garlic, very finely sliced
- 250 ml (8 fl oz) cider vinegar
- 750 g (1½ lb) granulated sugar
- 250 g (9 oz) stoned dates, finely chopped
- 100 g (4 oz) sultanas
- 50 g (2 oz) fresh ginger, peeled and grated
- ½ teaspoon salt
- ½ teaspoon ground allspice
- pinch of cayenne pepper

1. Peel, core and thinly slice the apples. Place in a large pan with the garlic and vinegar. Cook gently until the apples have broken down into a thick purée. Stir in the sugar, dates, sultanas, ginger, salt and spices. Cook for 20–25 minutes, stirring occasionally.

2. Spoon into hot, sterilized, glass preserving jars with clip tops. To enjoy the chutney at its best, store in a cool, dark, dry place for about 2–3 weeks before eating. This allows time for the flavours to mature. Once a jar has been opened, store in the fridge and eat within 1 month.

8   Meat Kebabs

9   Pasta Salad

Kebabs are a barbecue hit for more young men than older women and a great way of threading some favourite flavours on to one stick. Go for taste rather than looks, as different varieties of vegetable take different times to cook, leaving you with either raw onions and peppers or overcooked meat.

Spend a little more on buying tender pork fillet as this cut absorbs the Thai-flavoured marinade much better.

Thai Pork Kebabs   Makes 6 large kebabs

- 200 ml (7 fl oz) carton of coconut cream
- 1 heaped tablespoon Thai green curry paste (ready-made or see page 81)
- 2 teaspoons light muscovado sugar
- juice of $\frac{1}{2}$ lime
- 2 teaspoons Thai fish sauce or light soy sauce
- 800 g ($1\frac{3}{4}$ lb) lean pork (fillets are particularly tender or you could use pork steaks or thick boneless chops)
- 3 medium red onions, cut into 12–18 wedges
- 3 limes, cut into 12 wedges

6 long metal skewers

1. Mix together the coconut cream, curry paste, sugar, lime juice and fish or soy sauce in a non-metallic bowl. Cut the pork into about 2.5 cm (1 in) cubes and stir into the sauce. Leave to marinate in the fridge overnight or for about 2 hours at room temperature, stirring every so often.

2. To make up the kebabs, thread pieces of pork on to the skewers, alternating with red onion and lime wedges until all have been used up.

3. Place the kebabs over medium-hot coals for about 10 minutes, brushing generously with any marinade for the first 5 minutes, and turning every so often until golden and succulent.

There is nothing worse than overcooked pasta in a pasta salad. The dried varieties are better for salads as they absorb flavours and retain their texture. You can easily use leftover pasta from the night before, as long as you've kept it moist in the fridge with a little olive oil.

Minted Feta, Rocket and Olive Pasta Salad
Serves 6–8 as an accompaniment

- 350 g (12 oz) penne, rigatoni or other similar shaped pasta
- 8–10 large sprigs of mint, leaves removed, and chopped/torn if large
- 150 g (5 oz) frozen peas
- 200 g (7 oz) feta cheese, crumbled
- 50 g (2 oz) bag of rocket leaves
- grated zest and juice of 1 lemon
- flaked sea salt and freshly ground black pepper
- extra-virgin olive oil
- 20–30 good-quality marinated green olives, pitted

1. Cook the pasta in boiling salted water with 2 sprigs of the mint for the time given on the packet. Three minutes before the end of the cooking time, add the peas. Once the pasta and peas are cooked, drain in a colander and shake under cold running water until cool. Discard the mint sprigs.

2. Transfer to a large bowl and add the feta cheese, rocket, remaining mint, the lemon zest and half the juice, salt and pepper and a good glug of olive oil. Either roughly chop or smash the olives in a pestle and mortar and add to the pasta. Toss well and add more lemon juice, seasoning or olive oil, if preferred.

3. Pack in suitable containers for taking on a picnic or serve warm as part of a main course or starter with a barbecue.

depressed, even if I'm angry, I eat. Comfort eating solves everything.'

The two main ingredients of a dish that dashes the doldrums are fat and carbohydrate, and as we're much more health-conscious these days, our day-to-day diet tends to contain fewer of the so-called comfort foods. This means we view them as more of a treat and indulge only when we really need them. Everyone has their trigger points for turning to comfort foods – you might be cold and miserable, your partner may have dumped you, you might be short of money, nursing an enormous hangover, you might have had a terrible day at work, or feel fat and frumpy. All these emotions can be alleviated by a little treat – at least temporarily.

We're less likely to crave comfort foods in the summer, but that doesn't mean we need them only in winter. Although a wet and windy Sunday in February calls for a treat, scientific research has proved that stress is the main factor in consuming foods for comfort, no matter what time of year it is. However, our bodies crave sunlight in winter and this in turn sets off a chemical reaction that regulates our mood and appetite, tricking us into believing that we should consume more food and more calories.

As people have less time to cook at home, eating out has become less of a treat, so a home-cooked meal in a restaurant has enormous appeal. More and more restaurants, bars and pubs are serving up traditional dishes that we associate with comfort eating – things like sausage and mash, fish pie, simple pasta dishes and risotto, but also puddings such as bread and butter pudding, sticky toffee pudding and spotted dick with oodles of creamy, comforting custard.

Next time you're down in the dumps try cooking as therapy – you'll be surprised how the process can help relieve stress, and you'll also end up with a delicious comforting meal. And if you're cooking for two, what better way of cheering yourself and someone you love than by serving up a tasty treat?

1

Chocolate

Our survey showed that the older we become, the less likely we are to
be comforted by chocolate. However, there are obviously many who still
find it the most comforting food, whether it's a favourite chocolate bar, a
gooey cake, or a scrumptious choccy dessert.

Eating this pudding is like sinking into a warm bath at the end of a
traumatic day. The nutty nougat flavour of the Toblerone gives a rich,
saucy base to the light, airy topping, and the sauce oozes out when you
cut into it. You could use a Chocolate Orange instead, or just simple milk
chocolate broken into pieces if you prefer.

Soft Chocolate Toblerone Pudding   Serves 4–6

- 250 g (9 oz) Toblerone chocolate, broken into small pieces
- 300 ml (½ pint) milk
- 50 g (2 oz) unsalted butter, at room temperature
- 150 g (5 oz) light muscovado sugar
- 25 g (1 oz) cocoa powder
- 25 g (1 oz) self-raising flour
- 2 eggs, separated

approx. 1.5 litre (2½ pint) shallow ovenproof dish, greased with a little butter

1. Pre-heat the oven to 180°C/350°F/Gas Mark 4.

2. Place the pieces of Toblerone and the milk in a saucepan and gently heat until the chocolate has melted into the milk, then put to one side to cool slightly.

3. In a large bowl, beat together the butter and sugar with a wooden spoon. Sift in the cocoa powder and flour and add the egg yolks. Mix well and then pour in the chocolate milk, stirring until it's smooth.

4. Whisk the egg whites until they form soft peaks. This can be done using an electric hand whisk – just make sure you don't use too high a speed as the egg whites will become thick very quickly but won't hold a huge amount of air, which is what's needed for the pudding. Gently fold the whites into the chocolate mixture using a large metal spoon or spatula until totally mixed in.

5. Pour into the greased dish and sit inside a deep roasting tray. Pour enough hot water into the roasting tray to come halfway up the sides of the dish. Place in the oven and cook for 45 minutes until almost set; there should still be a slight wobble when the dish is lightly tapped. Remove the dish from the tray and leave to cool for about 5 minutes before serving as it is or with lots of cream or ice cream.

2   Cup of Tea

3   Toast

As a nation we are well known for our soothing brew. Nearly three times as many women as men take comfort in a cuppa with a cake or a biscuit, and in the North East of England it beat chocolate to the top of the poll.

Our lives have been transformed by tea-bags, but if you've got the time and the teapot for making the perfect cuppa, follow these simple steps and you'll really appreciate the effort.

Hot buttered toast is the kind of food you crave when you're on holiday abroad and just want good British bread and decent salty butter. It's been voted one of the most comforting snacks in the country, especially by those living in Scotland.

Try this eccentric variation where the contrast between a crispy outside and soft buttery inside is truly mind-blowing.

The Perfect Cuppa

1. Empty the kettle of any previously boiled water and fill with fresh (preferably filtered) water. Bring the kettle to the boil.

2. Warm a clean teapot with a little of the water just before it reaches boiling point, then swirl around and pour away.

3. Use tea leaves rather than bags for a fresh-flavoured tea – the type you use is up to you. Allow 1 teaspoon per person, plus one for the pot. Make sure the pot you're using has plenty of space for the tea to brew in the water.

4. Pour in the water as soon as it boils, taking the pot to the kettle so the water doesn't have a chance to cool down.

5. Cover the pot with a tea cosy (either one your Granny knitted or one of the cool, funky ones available now) and leave the tea to infuse for 3–4 minutes. Any longer and you'll ruin the true flavour of the tea, making it taste bitter.

6. When you're ready, pour the tea through a tea strainer (unless there's a mesh attached to your teapot) into sparkling clean mugs or cups and saucers.

7. When you add the milk depends on whether you're a MIF (milk-in-first) or TIF (tea-in-first) person, or maybe you prefer it black, with sugar, a slice of lemon or a sprig of mint.

8. Sit back and enjoy.

Soft Middle Toast   Serves 1

- 2 slices of medium cut bread
- good-quality softened butter (salted is best)

1. Place both slices of bread together in one side of your toaster, so the outside is golden and crispy but the inside is soft and steaming hot.

2. Spread the inside very generously with the butter. Press the buttered sides together and cut in half. The delicious, creamy, melted butter will ooze out of the soft centre when you bite into it, a sure guarantee you'll be back for more.

Try using a flavoured butter to spread on the inside of the toast. Refer to the recipe for Sweet Cinnamon Buttered Toast on page 16, or make your own flavoured butters using the suggestions below:

- roasted chopped nuts and maple syrup
- honey and ground ginger
- preserved ginger and ginger syrup
- vanilla extract and sugar

Alternatively, try some savoury versions which are great with bacon, sausages or scrambled, boiled or poached eggs:

- chopped fresh mixed herbs
- sun-dried tomato and garlic
- chopped chilli and chopped fresh coriander

4   Ice Cream

Under-35s, especially those who live in the North of England, are most likely to choose ice cream for its soothing qualities. Here, white chocolate and clotted cream are a heavenly match and the orange zest adds a suprising tang.

White Chocolate, Clotted Cream and Orange Ice Cream   Makes approx. 750 ml (1¼ pints)

- 350 ml (12 fl oz) milk
- 150 g (5 oz) white chocolate, broken into small pieces
- finely grated zest of 2 large oranges
- 5 egg yolks
- 100 g (4 oz) caster sugar
- 150 g (5 oz) clotted cream

1. Place the milk in a saucepan with the chocolate and orange zest. Stir until the chocolate has completely melted and the milk is at a simmer, but not boiling.

2. In a large bowl, whisk the egg yolks and sugar with an electric hand whisk until the mixture is light in colour and thick and creamy in texture.

3. Sit the bowl over a pan of gently simmering water, making sure it doesn't actually touch the water. Pour over the hot chocolate orange milk and stir until you have a tasty custard that is thick enough to coat the back of a wooden spoon. Be patient at this stage: it can take up to 30 minutes, but the result is well worth the wait. When it has thickened, remove from the heat and stir in the clotted cream, then leave to cool.

4. Once the mixture is cold, pour into an ice-cream machine and churn until it is thick and scoopable. This may need to be done in two stages, depending on the size of your machine. To enjoy the ice cream at its best, eat straight away after churning, and freeze any remaining mixture. If you're making the ice cream in advance, transfer to the freezer in a covered container. When you wish to serve it, remove from the freezer and keep at room temperature for 10 minutes, or transfer to the fridge 30 minutes beforehand to soften.

If you don't have an ice-cream machine, place the mixture in a container (preferably metal) and freeze, stirring well at hourly intervals. Eat when it's thick and scoopable or store in the freezer for no longer than 3 weeks to enjoy the ice cream at its best.

TIPS
For a really special treat, pour a good glug of your favourite liqueur over the softened ice cream just before eating. Cointreau, Grand Marnier or malt whisky work particularly well.

5

Sausage, Egg, Chips and Beans

You've been out on the town the night before and you wake up late craving carbohydrate and fat. What's the solution? A fry-up. Nearly half our voters chose sausage, egg, chips and beans as their favourite food to cure a hangover.

The Full English Breakfast on page 12 will give you the basic method, or this all-in-one version turns the ingredients into a soothing bake with a surprise in the centre, and is perfect served up with some home-made oven-baked chips.

Sausage, Bean and Egg Bake with Oven-baked Chips   Serves 3–4

- 6–8 good-quality thick pork sausages
- olive oil
- 1 onion, sliced
- 2 x 415 g (14 1/2 oz) tins of baked beans
- 1 teaspoon English mustard
- Worcestershire sauce
- large pinch of dried sage
- flaked sea salt and freshly ground black pepper
- 4 eggs

1. Pre-heat the oven to 200°C/400°F/Gas Mark 6.

2. Split the sausages open, peel away the skin and break the sausage meat into bite-size pieces.

3. Heat a little olive oil in a flameproof casserole and fry the onion for about 5 minutes. Add the sausages and fry with the onion for about 8 minutes until sizzling and cooked through. Stir in the tinned beans, mustard, a good shake of Worcestershire sauce and the sage, then season with plenty of pepper. Heat until the beans are just beginning to bubble.

4. With a spoon, make a well in the beans and break in an egg. Repeat with the other eggs, spacing them apart and adding a trickle of olive oil, salt and pepper on top of each. Place in the oven for about 15 minutes or until the egg whites are set. Serve straight away with either the fried Chips on page 70, or the Oven-baked Chips, right, which are lower in fat and really easy to prepare.

OVEN-BAKED CHIPS

- 4–6 large floury potatoes (depending on how hungry you are), such as Maris Piper, King Edward or Desiree
- olive oil
- flaked sea salt

1. Pre-heat the oven to 200°C/400°F/Gas Mark 6.

2. Peel the potatoes and cut them into long chip shapes; the size is entirely up to you, though finger-size is ideal. Rinse under the tap and pat dry with a tea towel. Place on a large baking sheet (preferably non-stick) and toss in a good glug of olive oil and sea salt. Shake the tray so the chips are in a flat layer and put in the oven. Cook for about 50 minutes, depending on the size, turning occasionally. When cooked they should be golden brown and crisp, with a light fluffy centre when broken open. Scatter with extra salt and serve straight away.

If you fancy adding some flavour to the chips, you can sprinkle them with a little ground spice, such as cayenne, paprika, mild chilli powder, cumin or coriander, or you could try garlic or celery salt.

6

Sausage and Mash

So trendy have sausage and mash become that they are even served up at wedding receptions. The Desperate Dan of comfort food is nearly three times as popular with men than with women, and is mostly consumed for comfort by Londoners.

This smashed mash recipe uses foil-baked spuds. The rough texture of the jacket potato mash helps to soak up the scrumptious, rich, fruity gravy. But we've also included a basic creamy mash for those who prefer a buttery, fluffy cloud of comfort with their bangers.

Bangers and Smashed Mash with Leek and Cider Gravy

Using tinned beef consommé or fresh beef stock gives you a far better flavoured gravy than instant stock cubes, and it really is worth keeping some in your cupboard/freezer for the times you're in need of some unexpected comfort.

- 2–3 large leeks
- 2 eating apples, peeled, cored
- 4 cloves of garlic, peeled but left whole
- few sprigs each of thyme, sage and rosemary
- olive oil
- 12 good-quality thick pork sausages
- flaked sea salt and freshly ground black pepper
- 500 ml (17 fl oz) cider
- 400 ml (14 fl oz) tinned beef consommé or fresh beef stock

POTATOES
- 8 medium–large floury potatoes, such as Maris Piper, King Edward or Desiree
- olive oil
- flaked sea salt and freshly ground black pepper
- salted butter
- a small handful of roughly chopped fresh herbs of your choice (e.g. parsley, basil, thyme or sage) or 1–2 teaspoons mustard (optional)

1. Pre-heat the oven to 200°C/400°F/Gas Mark 6.

2. Stab the potatoes several times with a fork and sit on a very large piece of aluminium foil. Pour over some olive oil and add plenty of salt. Wrap the foil loosely around the potatoes and fold over the edges to seal. Place in the oven and bake for 1¾ hours. Rather than baking, they will steam in the foil, giving a fluffy centre and soft skin.

3. While the potatoes are cooking, slice the leeks fairly thinly and wash well, getting rid of any grit. Scatter into a roasting tray with the apples, garlic and herbs. Pour over some olive oil and place the sausages on top. Season the whole lot with salt and pepper, then place in the oven for about 45 minutes, turning the sausages occasionally and moving the leeks around to prevent them from sticking. If they seem to be catching in the base of the pan, add a drop of the cider.

(CONTINUED OVERLEAF)

4. To check the potatoes are cooked, carefully open the foil and insert a sharp knife into a potato. If it comes out easily, they're done. If they still seem a little hard, put them back and check again after a further 10 minutes. Once they are cooked, remove them from the oven and keep warm in the foil for about 5 minutes, then tip into a large bowl. (For some, the best part of a potato is the skin, with its lovely nutty flavour. If you'd rather, you can easily peel it away before smashing the potatoes.) Roughly smash with a potato masher, adding plenty of butter (olive oil can be used as an alternative), herbs or mustard, if using, and seasoning, resulting in a very rustic-looking fluffy mash.

5. Take the roasting tray from the oven and place the sausages on serving plates with the potatoes and keep warm.

6. Remove the herb sprigs from the roasting tray and place the tray over a high heat. Add the cider and bring to the boil. When the cider has reduced by half, add the beef consommé or stock. Bring to the boil and cook for a few minutes until the quantity of gravy has reduced by about a third, giving you a rich, full-flavoured, loose gravy. Taste and add seasoning if it's needed. Spoon the gravy and leeks over the bangers and mash and tuck in.

TIP

Use 3 large sliced onions instead of the leeks, cooking them in exactly the same way.

Ultimate Creamy Mash

- 1.25 kg (2 ½ lb) large floury potatoes, such as Maris Piper, King Edward or Desiree
- salt and ground white pepper for a mash without any bits, but you can use freshly ground black pepper if you prefer
- 100 ml (3 ½ fl oz) single cream
- 75 g (3 oz) butter
- freshly grated nutmeg

1. Peel the potatoes and cut into large, equal-sized chunks. Place in a large saucepan and wash well in a few changes of cold water. Fill the pan with fresh water and add a good pinch of salt. Cover with a lid and bring to the boil. Having the lid on brings the water to the boil more quickly, ensuring even cooking of the potatoes. Keep an eye on the pan as the water will come over the sides once it reaches the boil. As soon as it's boiling, remove the lid and cook the potatoes for about 20–25 minutes or until they are tender (to check, insert the tip of a small sharp knife into a potato; they are done if they fall off easily). Make sure you don't overboil the potatoes as you'll have a soggy wet mash at the end.

2. Just before the potatoes are cooked, place the cream, butter and a good grating of nutmeg into a small pan and gently heat until the butter has melted.

3. Drain the potatoes in a colander and leave for a few minutes for the water to drain away completely and for some of the steam to evaporate. Tip back into the pan and mash with a traditional masher, adding the warm buttery cream as you go and mashing until the potato is really smooth. Season with salt and a little pepper and extra nutmeg if you want.

TIPS

You may prefer to use a potato ricer (looks like a large garlic press) or a mouli (mashes at the turn of a handle) instead of a traditional masher. You can make mashed potato the day before you need it: boil, drain and then mash the potatoes with a knob of butter and drop of milk to loosen. Transfer to a clean bowl and cover tightly with cling film. When needed, gently reheat the mash in a pan, stirring frequently, then stir in the warm buttery cream as before.

Try adding one or two of the following to the cream and butter, and remove before mashing:

- halved cloves of garlic
- bay leaves
- sprigs of thyme or rosemary

Or add these to the finished mash:

- wholegrain, Dijon or English mustard
- horseradish sauce/cream
- lightly fried spring onions
- caramelized onions (fry sliced onions gently in butter until golden and sticky)
- fried strips of bacon
- finely chopped black olives (watch the amount of salt added to the mash as olives are salty)
- grated Parmesan cheese and a drop of flavoured oil (truffle, rosemary or basil are good)
- diced cheese such as Gruyère, fontina or Gorgonzola (stir in briefly and allow to melt on your plate)
- chopped fresh herbs
- chopped roasted hazelnuts or walnuts

The list goes on, but try using flavours that complement the food you're serving with the mash.

7

Soup

One of the least guilt-inducing comfort foods, soup is favoured by both men and women and offers particular comfort in cold weather.

You can make soup out of almost anything in the fridge, but for solace and warmth tomato soup takes the biscuit. The tinned variety can be spruced up with a swirl of cream or a dash of sherry. This hearty home-made version is bursting with fresh vegetables and tomatoes, providing all the goodness you need when you're feeling low. Serve it with thick wedges of crusty bread to dunk in the soup or to wipe the bowl clean when you've finished.

Creamy Tomato Soup   Serves 4–6

- 3 tablespoons olive oil
- 1 large onion, chopped
- 2 cloves of garlic, crushed
- 2 sticks of celery, chopped
- 200 g (7 oz) carrots, chopped
- 1 bay leaf
- 1 large sprig of fresh thyme
- 750 g (1 ½ lb) ripe plum or vine-ripened tomatoes, roughly chopped
- ½ teaspoon sugar
- salt and freshly ground black pepper
- 200 ml (7 fl oz) passata
- 500 ml (17 fl oz) vegetable stock
- 100 ml (3 ½ fl oz) single cream
- splash of dry sherry
- crusty bread and butter, to serve

1. Heat the olive oil in a large saucepan and cook the onion for 5–6 minutes over a gentle heat until almost softened but not browned. Add the garlic, celery, carrots, bay leaf and thyme and cook for a further 6–7 minutes, stirring occasionally, making sure the vegetables don't stick to the base of the pan.

2. Add the chopped tomatoes and sugar and season well with salt and pepper. Cook for a few minutes, then stir in the passata and vegetable stock. Bring to a simmer, cover with a lid and cook for 35–40 minutes, until all the vegetables are tender.

3. Remove the bay leaf and thyme, then blend the soup in a liquidizer or food processor. This will probably have to be done in two batches. Pour the soup into a clean saucepan, passing it through a sieve if you want it really smooth. Stir in the cream, a splash of sherry and extra seasoning if required. Pour into large mugs or bowls and serve with fresh crusty buttered bread.

TIP

Any remaining soup will keep in the fridge for a few days or can be frozen in individual servings. When reheating, make sure it's heated thoroughly but don't boil it as this will ruin the taste and texture of the soup.

8   Fruit Crumble

If you like a walk in the countryside, plan a trip in September when the wild brambles are bursting with ripe blackberries. A home-made blackberry and apple crumble was more popular with men than with women in our survey. This classic pud can be adapted throughout the year to use whatever fruit is in season.

Blackberry and Bramley Apple Crunchy Crumble   Serves 4–6

FILLING
- 1 kg (2¼ lb) Bramley apples, peeled, quartered and cored
- 25 g (1 oz) butter
- 100 g (4 oz) caster sugar
- finely grated zest of 1 lemon
- 250 g (9 oz) blackberries

TOPPING
- 100 g (4 oz) plain white flour, sifted
- 100 g (4 oz) plain wholemeal flour
- 150 g (6 oz) unsalted butter
- 50 g (2 oz) flaked almonds, roughly crushed
- 75 g (3 oz) demerara sugar

approx. 1.5 litre (2½ pint) ovenproof dish, greased with a little butter

1. Pre-heat the oven to 200°C/400°F/Gas Mark 6.

2. First, make the filling. Cut each apple quarter into 3 wedges. Melt the butter in a large saucepan and add the apples, caster sugar and lemon zest. Cook over a medium heat for about 10 minutes until the apples begin to soften. Stir in the blackberries and then tip the mixture into the buttered dish.

3. To make the topping, combine the flours in a large bowl, then rub the butter into the flours until the mixture resembles coarse breadcrumbs. Stir in the almonds and sugar, then scatter over the filling.

4. Place in the oven for 20–25 minutes, until golden and crunchy. Serve hot with plenty of custard.

9   Sponge Pudding

It's dark and cold outside and the wind's howling. You're in need of something sweet and cheery – what better than steamed syrup sponge with lashings of custard?

Steamed Syrup Sponge   Serves 6

- 125 g (4½ oz) butter, at room temperature
- 125 g (4½ oz) caster sugar
- grated zest of 1 lemon or orange
- 3 eggs, beaten
- 125 g (4½ oz) self-raising flour, sifted
- 1 teaspoon baking powder
- 75 g (3 oz) fresh white fine breadcrumbs
- 5 tablespoons golden syrup

1.2 litre (2 pint) pudding basin, buttered and lightly floured

1. With an electric hand whisk or wooden spoon, beat together the butter, sugar and lemon or orange zest in a large bowl until light and fluffy. Gradually beat in the eggs, adding a little flour as you go, to prevent the mixture from curdling. Mix in the remaining flour with the baking powder, breadcrumbs and 2 tablespoons of the golden syrup.

2. Put the remaining golden syrup into the base of the pudding basin and spoon the sponge mixture over, levelling the top with the back of a wet spoon.

3. Cover the basin with a double piece of aluminium foil or greaseproof paper, with a pleat across the centre to allow space for the pudding to rise. Secure well by folding the foil around the edges and tying with a piece of string.

4. Place in a steamer over boiling water for 1½ hours, topping up the water frequently. To check if the pudding is cooked, pierce a skewer into the centre of the basin. If it comes out clean, the pudding is cooked.

5. Turn out the pudding on to a plate, making sure you scrape out any sticky syrup and spread it over the top. Serve straight away with custard and an extra drizzle of golden syrup.

10

Rice Pudding

Rice pudding lovers are split into two camps: those who like the skin and those who don't. If you don't, then you might as well stick to the tinned variety. But for those who like a spicy nutmeg crusty topping, here is the perfect recipe. Try it with a dollop of the Speedy Summerberry Jam on page 120.

Baked Creamy Rice Pudding   Serves 4–6

- 100 g (4 oz) short-grain pudding rice
- 450 ml (³/₄ pint) single cream
- 450 ml (³/₄ pint) full-fat milk
- 50 g (2 oz) caster sugar
- freshly grated nutmeg
- 1 vanilla pod (optional)
- 25 g (1 oz) unsalted butter

1.5 litre (2¹/₂ pint) ovenproof dish, greased with a little butter

1. Pre-heat the oven to 150°C/300°F/Gas Mark 2.

2. Rinse the rice under cold water and place in the ovenproof dish. Place the cream, milk, caster sugar and a generous grating of nutmeg in a medium saucepan. Scrape in the seeds of the vanilla pod, if using. Heat gently until almost simmering, then remove from the heat and pour over the rice, stirring well.

3. Dot the butter over the top and place in the oven for 1¹/₂ hours, stirring after the first 30 minutes (at this stage, you can add an extra grating of nutmeg, if liked). If the pudding still seems very runny, return to the oven, checking every 10 minutes, until it is loosely creamy but not runny. The cooking time will vary, depending on the type and depth of dish you use.

4. When the pudding is golden brown on top and has a soft, creamy texture, remove from the oven and allow to rest for 10 minutes before serving.

8: Nation's Favourite Afternoon Tea

Delicate bone china, lace tablecloths, dainty sandwiches, doilies and sugar tongs – these are all images associated with one of the most quintessential British traditions, afternoon tea. Nearly 21 per cent of you voted for the bastion of British teatime treats, the cream tea, comprising freshly baked golden scones, fruity strawberry jam and crusty clotted cream.

The recipe for clotted cream has remained unchanged for 400 years and, according to traditionalists, should be made with unpasteurized milk from Jersey cattle to ensure a rich golden crust. If you can't wait for someone to bring you back a tub from their holiday, you could always order it by post or try making it yourself, but you'll need ready access to fresh unpasteurized milk direct from the cow.

Clotted Cream (a traditional farmers' method)

Take a large pan of evening milk (richer than morning milk) direct from the cow and let it stand overnight. The next day, heat it slowly on the side of the range until it reaches about 80–85°C (176–185°F) and bubbles form around the outside. Take it off the stove and put the pan on a cool slate slab until the next day when the thick, rich, crusty cream can be skimmed off the top with a slotted spoon.

Afternoon tea developed as a ritual in England around the 1840s and the tradition has been attributed to Anna Maria, the wife of the seventh Duke of Bedford. Supposedly suffering from a 'sinking feeling' in the afternoon due to the long wait between lunch and dinner, she summoned her housemaid to bring her some tea and something to eat. She soon began to invite a small and select circle of ladies to join her and it became a daily occurrence at Woburn Abbey. By the end of the century afternoon tea had become an institution across the land, crossing all ages and class barriers.

In Victorian times, women were required to wear tea dresses to attend an afternoon tea party. There are few occasions these days that dictate a particular dress code for taking tea – unless you should have the good fortune to be invited by

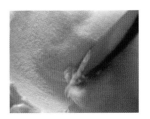

The Queen for tea at Buckingham Palace. For The Queen's three annual garden parties, Twinings tea is served in the tea tent alongside an array of crustless cucumber or egg and cress sandwiches, tiny slices of battenburg, Swiss roll and chocolate eclairs with the obligatory scones with jam and clotted cream, again in miniature form. In total they serve around 40,000 sandwiches, 6,000 scones, 2,500 eclairs and 27,000 cups of tea to the 8,000 guests.

Regional variations on teatime treats are endless – lardy cake in the South, Eccles cakes and fat rascals in the north, scones or Devonshire splits in the South West, potato scones and Dundee cake in Scotland, bara brith in Wales and barmbrack in Ireland. But forget the Victoria sandwich, Battenburg or iced fancies; according to our survey, afternoon tea should now include chocolate brownies and doughnuts – not the least bit authentic in some people's eyes.

Food writer Madhur Jaffrey grew up in India where afternoon tea was considered a very British affair, with a few unusual additions: 'My mother would of course pour, and there'd be a proper Wedgwood tea-set, that was essential. But what we would serve would be everything that the English would have, which would be cakes and pastries and tea with milk and sugar, plus we'd have the Indian side which would be samosas or all kinds of other very spicy things.'

Whether or not you partake in this afternoon ritual, there's no denying that tea is one of Britain's great institutions.

1

Scones with Jam and Clotted Cream

The traditional Devon or Cornwall cream tea is equally popular with men and women, especially for those aged between 35 and 44. There's often a debate about the etiquette of scones with jam and clotted cream: which comes first, the jam or the cream? Some say it depends whether you're from Devon or Cornwall, but it seems no matter where you live it's down to personal taste.

Zesty Scones   Makes approx. 8

- 350 g (12 oz) self-raising flour
- 1½ teaspoons baking powder
- pinch of salt
- 40 g (1½ oz) caster sugar
- 75 g (3 oz) unsalted butter, slightly softened
- 1 teaspoon freshly grated lemon zest
- 175 ml (6 fl oz) milk
- flour for dusting, or 1 small egg beaten with ½ teaspoon sugar for brushing

1. Pre-heat the oven to 220°C/425°F/Gas Mark 7.

2. Sift the flour, baking powder and salt into a bowl, then stir in the sugar. Add the butter and rub it in, giving a texture of fine breadcrumbs, then stir in the lemon zest. Gradually add the milk and mix to give a soft, smooth dough, kneading lightly with floured hands. If the dough feels a little dry, add a drop more milk.

3. On a lightly floured surface, roll out the scone mixture to 2.5 cm (1 in) thick. Using a 7.5 cm (3 in) plain or fluted pastry cutter, press firmly through the dough, trying not to twist the cutter or you'll end up with unevenly risen scones when they're cooked. Place onto a greased baking sheet and continue with the rolled dough. Lightly knead any trimmings and cut out as many scones as possible until all of the dough is used up. Dust the scones with a little flour for a matt finish, or brush with the beaten egg and sugar for a shiny glaze.

4. Bake in the oven for 12–15 minutes until golden and nicely risen. Once cooked, place on a wire rack to cool slightly. These scones are definitely best served still warm from the oven with lots of melting butter or strawberry jam and sticky clotted cream.

TIPS
If you prefer perfectly plain scones, just leave out the lemon zest; but do try it for a change as the lemon is really refreshing with the strawberry jam and cream.
For a fruit scone, add 75 g (3 oz) sultanas to the mixture before adding the milk. Orange zest instead of lemon is especially good with sultanas.

2

Carrot Cake

Carrot cake is the favourite afternoon treat for vegetarians and is three times more popular in Wales than in the North East of England.

During the Second World War, carrots were used to give flavour, texture and sweetness to cakes when other more usual ingredients were sparse. Whether the carrot cake dates back to the 1940s is difficult to say, but it's certainly beaten some of the more traditional cakes and sponges into the nation's top ten teatime treats.

Moist Carrot Cake with Coconut Orange Cream

- 150 ml (¼ pint) sunflower oil
- 100 g (4 oz) soft light brown sugar
- 2 eggs, lightly beaten
- 75 g (3 oz) golden syrup
- 175 g (6 oz) wholemeal self-raising flour
- 1 level teaspoon ground cinnamon
- ½ teaspoon ground allspice
- ½ teaspoon ground ginger
- 1 teaspoon bicarbonate of soda
- 200 g (7 oz) finely grated carrots
- 75 g (3 oz) sultanas
- 25 g (1 oz) desiccated coconut

1 x 18 cm (7 in) round or square cake tin, greased, and the base lined with greaseproof paper

TOPPING
- 2 tablespoons fine-cut orange marmalade
- 150 g (5 oz) cream cheese
- 50 ml (2 fl oz) coconut cream
- 40 g (1½ oz) icing sugar
- freshly grated nutmeg or ground cinnamon, to finish

1. Pre-heat oven to 160°C/325°F/Gas Mark 3.

2. In a large bowl or electric mixer, whisk together the oil, sugar, eggs and golden syrup until totally combined. Mix in the remaining cake ingredients and pour into the prepared tin.

3. Bake in the oven for 45 minutes for a round cake, or 30 minutes for the square, until nicely risen and firm but springy when lightly pressed. Insert a skewer through the centre if you're not sure – if it comes out clean, the cake is ready. Leave the cake to cool in the tin for 10 minutes before turning out onto a wire rack to cool completely.

4. While the cake is cooling, make the topping. Warm the marmalade in a microwave or small saucepan until melted. Beat it into the cream cheese with the coconut cream and icing sugar. Place in the fridge to firm up, and when cold spread over the cooled cake.

5. For a final touch, grate over some nutmeg or dust with some ground cinnamon. Because the carrot cake has been made using oil, it will stay moist for quite a few days in an airtight container if you can bear not to eat it all straightaway.

3   Chocolate Cake

Favoured by the under-25s, chocolate cake has made a relatively recent entry onto the menu for afternoon tea. Coffee and walnut cake, Victoria sponge (often referred to as Victoria sandwich) or a hearty slice of fruit cake would be more authentic, but this light, moist chocolate cake with a rich, malty flavour is delicious with a hot cup of freshly brewed tea and would even work with a few fresh strawberries on the side. The cake has two fillings for a really indulgent afternoon treat, but if you don't want to be so extravagant, just choose one.

Malted Chocolate Fudge Cake

- 175 g (6 oz) self-raising flour
- 2 tablespoons cocoa powder
- 3 heaped tablespoons Ovaltine
- 1 teaspoon baking powder
- 1 teaspoon bicarbonate of soda
- 150 g (5 oz) caster sugar
- 2 tablespoons golden syrup
- 2 eggs, lightly beaten
- 150 ml (¼ pint) milk
- 150 ml (¼ pint) corn oil
- icing sugar, for dusting

FILLING ONE
- 150 g (5 oz) plain chocolate, broken into pieces
- 15 g (½ oz) butter
- 120 ml (4 fl oz) double cream

FILLING TWO
- 150 ml (¼ pint) double cream
- 1½ tablespoons Ovaltine

2 x 20 cm (8 in) sandwich cake tins, greased and dusted with flour

1. Pre-heat the oven to 160°C/325°F/Gas Mark 3.

2. Sift together the flour, cocoa powder, Ovaltine, baking powder and bicarbonate of soda in a large mixing bowl. Add the remaining ingredients and beat well to give a smooth consistency.

3. Divide the mixture between the cake tins and bake in the oven for 30–35 minutes, until just firm to the touch. Leave to cool in the tins for about 10 minutes before turning out onto a wire rack. While the cake is cooling, make the fillings.

4. Start with filling one. Place the chocolate and butter in a bowl over a pan of gently simmering water and leave to slowly melt. Stir in the cream and remove from the heat. Leave to cool until it is a spreadable consistency, then spread over the base sponge.

5. For filling two, lightly whip the cream with the Ovaltine until it forms soft peaks. Spread over the chocolate filling and top with the remaining sponge. Dust with icing sugar and the gooey cake is ready to serve.

8   Biscuits

Dunking a digestive into a mug of tea is alright for elevenses, but the etiquette of afternoon tea requires more refined behaviour. These crumbly, buttery shortbreads would grace any afternoon tea table.

Lemon and Passion Fruit Shortbread Biscuits   Makes approx. 16

- 225 g (8 oz) unsalted butter, at room temperature
- 75 g (3 oz) caster sugar
- 275 g (10 oz) plain flour, sifted
- pinch of salt
- 75 g (3 oz) fine semolina
- 1 teaspoon grated lemon zest
- flesh and seeds from 1 ripe passion fruit
- extra caster sugar, for dusting

1. Pre-heat the oven to 160°C/325°F/Gas Mark 3.

2. In a large bowl, beat together the butter and caster sugar until the mixture turns a lighter colour and is creamy in consistency. This can be done with just a wooden spoon rather than an electric mixer. Beat in the flour, salt, semolina, lemon zest and passion fruit, then use your hands to form a pliable dough.

3. On a floured surface, roll the dough with your hands into a long sausage shape, roughly 5 cm (2 in) in diameter. Wrap in cling film and put in the fridge to firm up for about 45 minutes. If the mixture seems particularly soft, wrap it in cling film before rolling and put in the fridge for about 30 minutes. Then roll it as above.

4. Once chilled, cut 1 cm (½ in) thick rounds with a sharp knife, trying not to put too much pressure on the dough or you'll end up with a flat edge to the biscuits.

5. Place the rounds on a couple of greased baking sheets and bake in the oven for about 35 minutes until lightly golden. Lift gently from the tray and sprinkle with caster sugar. Once they're cool, enjoy straight away or store in an airtight container.

TIP

For a variation in flavour, why not try these suggestions as an alternative to the lemon and passion fruit:
- **1 teaspoon grated orange or lime zest**
- **1 teaspoon vanilla extract**
- **1 teaspoon almond essence**
- **2 teaspoons chopped stem ginger**

9   Doughnuts

Ring doughnuts, cinnamon doughnuts, apple, cream or jam. They have no history of belonging to traditional afternoon tea, but now twice as many men prefer them to women and they're fifteen times more popular in Wales than they are in Northern Ireland.

Doughnuts are surprisingly easy to make at home and delicious when still warm. Don't be put off by the deep-frying as it's wonderfully satisfying to watch the raw dough puff up into golden fluffy doughnuts.

Cinnamon Sugared Doughnut Rings
Makes approx. 14–16

- 2 eggs
- 100 g (4 oz) caster sugar
- 100 ml (3 $^1/_2$ fl oz) soured cream
- 350 g (12 oz) plain flour
- 2 $^1/_2$ teaspoons baking powder
- 1 teaspoon bicarbonate of soda
- $^1/_2$ teaspoon salt
- $^1/_2$ teaspoon ground cinnamon
- oil for deep-frying
- 4 tablespoons caster sugar mixed with 1 teaspoon ground cinnamon

1. Whisk together the eggs and sugar until frothy, then stir in the soured cream. Sift in the flour, baking powder, bicarbonate of soda, salt and cinnamon. Mix until everything comes together in the bowl into a sticky dough. Transfer to a lightly floured surface and knead briefly with your hands until the dough becomes soft and smooth in texture.

2. Using a little more flour if you need to, roll the dough until it's about 5 mm ($^1/_4$ in) thick. Cut out circles in the dough with a pastry cutter, approximately 7.5–9 cm (3–3 $^1/_2$ in) diameter. In the centre of each one cut a smaller circle approximately 2.5 cm (1 in) in diameter. Transfer the rings and centre circles to a piece of greaseproof paper and roll out any trimmings, repeating until all the dough is used.

3. Heat plenty of oil in a deep-fat fryer or saucepan to 180°C/350°F. If you don't have a thermometer, drop a 2–3 cm ($^3/_4$–1 $^1/_4$ in) cube of bread into the hot oil. If it sizzles straight away and becomes golden in about a minute, the temperature is fine.

4. Drop a few doughnut rings and the centre circles into the oil and fry until golden on both sides (about 2 minutes). Once cooked, drain on kitchen paper to absorb excess fat, then toss in the sugar and cinnamon. The easiest way to do this is to use a large plastic sandwich bag to shake around a few doughnuts at a time so they get an even coating of cinnamon sugar.

It's best to eat the doughnuts while they're still warm, or at least within a few hours of making them, but you won't be able to resist the bite-sized centres just as soon as they're cool enough to handle.

10

Sandwiches

The modern sandwich is named after the fourth Earl of Sandwich who liked a slice of beef between two pieces of toasted bread. The sandwich has now become a veritable feast of flavours, but try these modern alternatives for a 21st-century afternoon-tea treat.

Smoked Salmon and Dill Butter Tea-Sandwich
Makes 16 sandwich triangles

- 65 g (2½ oz) softened butter
- 1 heaped tablespoon fresh dill, chopped
- good squeeze of lemon juice
- salt and pepper
- 8 thin slices white or brown bread
- 4–8 slices of smoked salmon, depending on size
- ¼ cucumber, peeled and thinly sliced

1. Mix together the butter, dill and a squeeze of lemon juice. Season with salt and pepper, then spread onto the 8 slices of bread. Place a slice of smoked salmon and some sliced cucumber on top of 4 pieces and top with the remaining slices of bread.

2. Trim away the crusts and cut each into 4 triangles. Arrange on an elegant platter with some wedges of lemon for decoration.

Ham, Watercress and Mustardy Cream Cheese Sandwich
Makes 12 sandwich fingers

- 120 g (4½ oz) cream cheese
- ¾ teaspoon English mustard
- salt and pepper
- 8 thin slices of wholemeal bread
- 8 slices of cooked ham
- 1 small bunch watercress

1. Mix together the cream cheese and the mustard and season with salt and pepper. Add extra mustard for a more fiery flavour; however, it's probably best to have a mild mustard flavour for afternoon tea.

2. Spread the cream cheese mixture on the 8 slices of bread and place the ham on top of 4. Divide the watercress into small sprigs and place on top. Finish with the remaining slices of bread, trim off the crusts and cut each into 3 fingers. Serve on a pretty plate with some extra sprigs of watercress.

Pancetta-wrapped Prunes and Sausages

Makes 16

- 16 dried, ready-to-eat prunes
- 16 good-quality cocktail sausages (try some herb-flavoured ones)
- 16 slices of pancetta (if unavailable, use thinly sliced streaky bacon)
- olive oil

1. Pre-heat the oven to 200°C/400°F/Gas Mark 6.

2. Split the prunes down one side to open them up, wrap each one around a cocktail sausage and then wrap a piece of pancetta around each prune to secure. These can be placed in the fridge until needed or cooked straight away.

3. Sit on a baking tray, drizzle with a little oil and roast for about 12-15 minutes until golden and crispy, turning occasionally to get an even colour.

↓ continued

Spiced Red Cabbage with Cranberry Sauce

Serves 6-8

The brilliant colour and festive flavour of this dish is perfect for the Christmas table. The great thing about it is that it can be made 2-3 days before the big day and gently reheated when needed.

- 1 medium-large red cabbage
- 75 g (3 oz) butter
- 1 red onion, sliced
- 2 Granny Smith apples, peeled, cored and sliced
- 1 tablespoon soft dark brown sugar
- 3 tablespoons red wine vinegar
- 4 tablespoons cranberry sauce
- 2 cinnamon sticks, broken in half
- 4 whole cloves
- 200 ml (7 fl oz) cranberry or apple juice

1. Cut the cabbage into quarters and remove the white core, then slice the red parts of the cabbage fairly thinly.

2. Melt the butter in a medium flameproof casserole or a saucepan. Gently fry the onion for about 5 minutes and then add the remaining ingredients, including the cabbage. Cover the pan and cook over a low-moderate heat for about 50 minutes-1 hour or until the cabbage is tender and all the liquid has evaporated, stirring occasionally. If the cabbage is cooked but there's too much liquid in the base of the pan, remove the lid, increase the heat slightly and continue to cook until it's almost evaporated. But keep the cabbage fairly moist, especially if you plan on preparing it in advance.

Rich Bread Sauce

Serves 6–8

- 10 whole cloves
- 1 large onion, cut in half
- 2 bay leaves
- flaked sea salt
- 1 blade of mace or
- ½ teaspoon freshly grated nutmeg
- 10 black peppercorns
- 600 ml (1 pint) full-fat milk
- 100 g (4 oz) white breadcrumbs, from a 2-day-old loaf, crusts removed
- 25 g (1 oz) butter
- 4–6 tablespoons double cream

1. Press the cloves into the 2 onion halves and place in a saucepan with the bay leaves, pinch of salt, blade of mace or nutmeg, peppercorns and milk. Bring to the boil and then remove from the heat, cover with a lid and leave in a warm place to infuse for about 30 minutes–1 hour.

2. Return the pan to the heat and stir in the breadcrumbs. Bring the sauce to a simmer and cook on a low heat for about 20 minutes until it's creamy and thickened.

3. The bread sauce can be made a couple of days in advance, kept in the fridge and rewarmed, or served straight away. Just before serving, remove the onion, bay leaves, peppercorns and mace and briskly stir in the butter and double cream to give a wonderful rich, creamy sauce.

Apple, Cranberry and Chestnut Stuffing

Serves 6–8

- 25 g (1 oz) butter
- 2 large red onions, chopped
- 100 g (4 oz) breadcrumbs
- 2 Granny Smith apples, peeled and coarsely grated
- 200 g (7 oz) cooked and peeled chestnuts (a box of vacuum-packed ones is ideal), roughly chopped
- 450 g (1 lb) good-quality pork sausage meat
- 75 g (3 oz) dried cranberries
- finely grated zest of 1 lemon
- a handful of sage leaves, chopped, plus a few extra whole leaves
- flaked sea salt and freshly ground black pepper
- large knob of butter

1. Pre-heat the oven to 200°C/400°F/Gas Mark 6.

2. Melt the butter in a frying pan and gently fry the onions until softened. Remove from the pan and leave to cool.

3. In a large bowl, mix the breadcrumbs, grated apple, chestnuts, sausage meat, cranberries, lemon zest, chopped sage and cooled onions and season well with salt and pepper. Stir really well for a couple of minutes with a wooden spoon or, if you can bear it, with clean hands, getting plenty of air into the mixture which will give you a really light stuffing when cooked. A good tip to check if you have enough seasoning in the stuffing is to fry a spoonful for a couple of minutes to check it tastes okay, adding extra seasoning or sage if necessary.

4. Spoon the stuffing into a medium-sized greased ovenproof dish, letting it fall into place rather than pressing with the spoon. Arrange a few whole sage leaves on top and dot with butter. It's now ready to be cooked for 30–40 minutes until crispy and golden on top. The stuffing can easily be made the day before and kept in the fridge overnight.

2 Hot Cross Buns

Over a third of vegetarians voted this Easter speciality their favourite festive food, above Christmas pudding, Christmas cake and mince pies.

Home-made hot cross buns are much nicer than bought ones, and because Easter comes but once a year, it's worth going to the extra effort of making them. Rather than the traditional sugar and water glaze to finish the buns, these have a sticky orange glaze that adds an extra fruity flavour and a brilliant shine.

Hot Cross Buns   Makes 12

- 450 g (1 lb) plain flour, plus extra for dusting
- 1 teaspoon salt
- ½ teaspoon ground cinnamon
- 1½ teaspoons mixed spice
- 50 g (2 oz) butter
- 75 g (3 oz) currants
- 50 g (2 oz) mixed peel, chopped
- 7 g sachet or 1½ teaspoons fast-action dried yeast
- 100 ml (3½ fl oz) warm water
- 100 ml (3½ fl oz) warm milk
- 1 egg, beaten

DECORATION
- 100 g (4 oz) ready-made shortcrust pastry or 100 g (4 oz) plain flour mixed with 3 tablespoons water to give a dough
- 1 egg, beaten
- 2 tablespoons freshly squeezed orange juice, strained through a sieve
- 2 tablespoons granulated sugar

1. Sift the flour, salt, cinnamon and mixed spice into a large bowl (or into a large bowl for an electric mixer with a dough hook) and rub in the butter. Stir in the currants, mixed peel and yeast. Make a well in the centre and pour in the water, milk and beaten egg. Mix this together to form a sticky dough, then knead on a floured surface for 8–10 minutes (or for 5 minutes in the machine on a low speed) until it's smooth and elastic. Place the dough in a large bowl, greased lightly with oil, cover with a slightly damp tea towel and leave to rise in a warm place for about an hour, or until doubled in volume.

2. Knock back the dough by pressing the air out of it, and knead for a couple of minutes. Divide into 12 equal-sized pieces and shape into round buns. Place on to 1 or 2 large greased baking sheets, leaving enough space between each bun for rising. Cover with the tea towel and leave to rise again until doubled in size, which will take about 30–45 minutes.

3. Pre-heat the oven to 200°C/400°F/Gas Mark 6.

4. While the buns are rising, roll out the pastry or flour dough thinly and cut out 24 strips, approx. 5 mm x 7.5 cm (¼ in x 3 in), for the decoration.

5. Brush the risen buns with the beaten egg and lay 2 strips of the pastry/dough on to each bun to form a cross in the middle. Brush with the egg and place in the oven. Cook for 15–18 minutes until golden and hollow-sounding when tapped underneath.

6. While the buns are cooking, place the orange juice and sugar in a small saucepan and gently heat until the sugar has dissolved.

7. As soon as the buns are out of the oven, brush with the glaze and eat straight away, or leave to cool on a wire rack and serve toasted, dripping with butter.

TIP
If you want to use fresh yeast, stir 25 g (1 oz) into the warm milk and water until dissolved, then carry on as above, mixing the liquid into the dried ingredients with the beaten egg.

3

Christmas Pudding

If the guests around your Christmas table are over 55 and from the Midlands, they're much more likely to enjoy the Christmas pud.

Puddings are best made in October or November to allow time for the fruits to mature, though they're still wonderful if made at the last minute. If you are making them in advance, be sure to store them tightly wrapped in greaseproof paper and parchment or foil in a cool, dry place.

Grandma's Rich Christmas Pud
Makes 3 x 900 g (2 lb) or 2 x 1.5 kg (3 lb) puds

- 50 g (2 oz) self-raising flour
- 175 g (6 oz) plain flour
- 1 teaspoon baking powder
- 1/2 teaspoon freshly grated nutmeg
- 1 teaspoon mixed spice
- 50 g (2 oz) ground almonds
- 225 g (8 oz) shredded suet
- 225 g (8 oz) dark muscovado sugar
- 100 g (4 oz) white breadcrumbs from a 2-day-old loaf
- 1.5 kg (3 lb) mixed currants, raisins and sultanas
- 1 tablespoon black treacle
- finely grated zest and juice of 1 lemon
- finely grated zest of 1 orange
- 1 medium carrot, finely grated
- 1 medium cooking apple, peeled and grated
- 2 tablespoons brandy or rum, plus extra for flaming
- 150 ml (5 fl oz) dark ale or stout
- 4 eggs, beaten
- flour and butter, for preparing the basins

1. Sift together the flours, baking powder and spices into a large bowl. Stir in the almonds, suet, sugar and breadcrumbs, mixing well. Add the remaining pudding ingredients, stirring well after each addition. Cover with cling film and leave in the fridge or a really cool place for 24 hours or up to 1 week if possible, stirring a few times.

2. Grease and lightly flour either 3 x 900 ml (1 1/2 pint) or 2 x 1.2 litre (2 pint) basins and pack in the pudding mixture. Top the surface of the puddings with a circle of greaseproof paper, then cover with baking parchment or aluminium foil. Fold around the edges of the basin and tie with string, or tightly scrunch the foil under the lip of the basin. Place in a steamer over boiling water for about 6 hours, topping up with water every so often, making sure it doesn't boil away (if you don't have a steamer, you can place the pudding on an upturned bowl in the bottom of a saucepan).

3. Leave to cool and remove the parchment/foil and greaseproof paper and replace with a new lot. The puddings can now be stored in a cool, dry place. On the big day the pudding should be steamed for about 1 1/2 – 2 hours, or covered loosely and heated in the microwave for about 6 minutes on high power, checking its progress every so often by inserting a skewer into the centre and leaving for a couple of seconds. If the skewer comes out piping hot, the pudding is ready to eat after standing for 1 minute. For more accurate timings it's best to check the manufacturer's instructions.

4. To flame the pudding, half-fill a metal ladle with brandy (or use as much as you want) and carefully heat over a gas flame or lit candle. When the flame is hot enough, the brandy will light. Pour the flaming brandy over the pudding. Make sure the lights are out when taking to the table for a grand entrance. A word of advice: if you have a piece of holly on top, watch it doesn't catch alight.

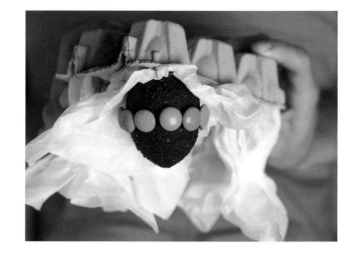

Chocolate Eggs

There used to be a great tradition of making eggs for Easter, usually of the painted or decorated hard-boiled variety. Voters in Northern Ireland and Wales have a sweeter tooth than those in the rest of the country, where 37 per cent said chocolate Easter eggs were their favourite festive food. These chocolate eggs are easy for the kids to make and would be perfect to hand out as Easter pressies.

Chocolate Refrigerator Eggs   Makes 6

- 150 g (5 oz) dark chocolate, broken into pieces
- 2 tablespoons golden syrup
- 2 tablespoons cocoa powder
- 100 g (4 oz) butter
- ½ teaspoon finely grated orange zest
- 225 g (8 oz) digestive biscuits, finely crushed

OPTIONAL DECORATIONS

- 1 empty egg box
- tissue paper
- ribbon
- Smarties or alternative sweets
- melted chocolate

1. Place the chocolate, golden syrup, cocoa powder and butter in a saucepan and gently heat until melted. Stir in the orange zest and crushed digestives, then mix well.

2. Leave the mixture to cool for about 10 minutes, or until cool enough to handle, then firmly shape into neat eggs using your hands to mould. Sit in an egg box loosely lined with cling film and put in the fridge to set for about 30 minutes.

3. The eggs can now be individually wrapped in tissue paper, tied with coloured ribbon, or decorated with Smarties or other decorations stuck on with some melted chocolate.

TIPS

Additional flavours can be added to the eggs: **50 g (2 oz) sultanas, raisins or chopped dried apricots, or 50 g (2 oz) finely chopped nuts, such as walnuts, pecans, hazelnuts or Brazil nuts.**

It appears the mince pie appreciation society has its home in the South West of England, as one in three people in that region put these spicy pies at the top of their Christmas list. You could cheat and buy ready-made pastry as well as a jar of mincemeat, but if you consider Christmas to be the biggest event in the culinary calendar, have a go at making this rich, crispy pastry flavoured with a touch of orange and mixed spice.

Deep-filled Mince Pies with Spiced Orange Pastry   Makes 12

- 350 g (12 oz) plain flour, sifted, plus extra for rolling
- 2 teaspoons mixed spice, plus an extra pinch for dusting
- pinch of salt
- 175 g (6 oz) fridge-cold butter, diced
- 75 g (3 oz) icing sugar, plus extra for dusting
- 3 teaspoons finely grated orange zest, plus 12 twists of orange zest to decorate
- 2 small eggs
- 1 tablespoon water or milk
- 600 g (1 lb 5 oz) good-quality mincemeat

TO GLAZE

1 small egg, beaten, or milk

1 or 2 deep muffin tins

1. Pre-heat the oven to 190°C/375°F/Gas Mark 5.

2. To make the pastry, place the flour, mixed spice, salt and butter in a food processor and process until it resembles coarse breadcrumbs. Add the icing sugar and grated orange zest, then blitz briefly. With

the machine running, add the eggs and water or milk, and pulse the processor until the mixture comes together in a ball. If the pastry seems a little dry, add another tablespoon of water or milk. Tip on to a floured surface and very gently knead until just smooth. Don't over-knead at this point or the pastry will become tough when cooked. Wrap in cling film and leave in the fridge for about 30 minutes to firm up and relax.

3. On a lightly floured surface, roll out three quarters of the pastry to about 3 mm (⅛ in) thick. Using a 10 cm (4 in) plain pastry cutter, cut out 12 circles of pastry. Lightly press into the muffin tins to fit neatly in the holes. Divide the mincemeat between the pastry (about 1 tablespoon each). Roll out the remaining pastry to the same thickness and cut out 12 circles using a 7.5 cm (3 in) cutter. Dampen the edges of the pastry in the tins with water and sit the smaller circles on

top, pressing the edges together lightly to seal.

4. Brush the tops with the beaten egg or milk glaze and bake in the oven for 20–25 minutes until golden. Once the pies are cooked, leave in the tins for 5 minutes and then carefully transfer them to a wire rack and leave to cool.

5. Serve warm, dusted with icing sugar and mixed spice and decorated with a twist of orange zest. A good spoonful of Brandy Butter (see page 154) makes a fine accompaniment.

TIP
If you're using bought mincemeat, go for the best quality possible. Have a taste and add any extras if you want to, such as a splash of brandy, whisky, rum, grated lemon or orange zest, finely chopped nuts, finely chopped dried apricots, prunes or dates, or orange marmalade.

At number six in the festive top ten, roast lamb is preferred by those born between 1949 and 1958. You can follow the recipes for Roast Lemon and Thyme Lamb (see page 46) or Roast Shoulder of Lamb (see page 28). Whichever recipe you choose, these three sauces will marry perfectly with the succulent meat.

Mint Sauce

Serves 4–6

- 2 large handfuls of fresh mint leaves, finely chopped
- 2 tablespoons cider vinegar
- 2 tablespoons apple juice
- 1 tablespoon caster sugar

Mix together all the ingredients and leave to infuse for about an hour before serving.

TIP

If you're having this mint sauce in the spring or summer months, add 2 tablespoons finely chopped spring onions for a change.

Redcurrant Sauce

Makes about 400 ml [14 fl oz]

Redcurrants are a classic accompaniment to roast lamb, and are usually eaten as a jelly. This recipe is really quick to prepare and tastes great. The seasonal availability of redcurrants is limited to August and September, so buy in bulk and stick them in the freezer.

- 450 g (1 lb) fresh or frozen redcurrants
- 300 g (11 oz) soft light brown sugar
- couple of pieces of peeled orange zest
- 1 shallot, finely chopped
- 100 ml (3½ fl oz) port
- 2 sprigs of rosemary

Place all the ingredients in a saucepan and bring to a simmer. Cook gently for about 20 minutes until you have a loose jam consistency. Discard the rosemary and orange zest and leave to cool to room temperature. This will keep in the fridge for up to a month.

Creamy Roast Onion and Rosemary Sauce

Serves 6

A perfect sauce to serve with lamb, particularly as the oven is already at full blast for the meat.

- 3 large onions, thickly sliced
- 50 g (2 oz) butter
- flaked sea salt and freshly ground black pepper
- 4 sprigs of rosemary
- 450 ml (¾ pint) milk
- 2 tablespoons cornflour mixed with 2 tablespoons water

1. Pre-heat the oven to 200°C/400°F/Gas Mark 6 (it should already be at this temperature if you are following the roast lamb recipes).

2. Place the onions in a medium-sized roasting tray with the butter and season with salt and pepper. Place in the oven for 40 minutes until cooked and beginning to go slightly golden, turning occasionally in the tray.

3. As soon as the onions are in the oven, place the rosemary in a saucepan with the milk. Gently bring to the boil, then remove from the heat. This allows the rosemary flavour to infuse into the milk.

4. Just before the onions are done, stir the cornflour mixture into the rosemary-infused milk. Place the pan back on to the heat and bring to a gentle simmer, cooking for a couple of minutes until thickened slightly. Remove the rosemary and pour the sauce into a food processor or liquidizer. Take the onions from the oven and add to the sauce. Blitz until smooth, season with salt and pepper and either serve straight away or gently reheat when needed.

7

Christmas Cake

A quarter of the over-55s who voted in our survey put Christmas cake at **the top of their list**. The secret of a rich, moist cake is to make it as early as possible (start in October or November) as the flavour improves with keeping. Then all you have to do is decorate it up to a week before the big day. Marzipan or almond paste and icing are traditional, or you can arrange whole blanched almonds on top of the cake before you bake it.

Fruity Christmas Cake

- 300 g (11 oz) currants
- 200 g (7 oz) raisins
- 200 g (7 oz) sultanas
- 200 g (7 oz) dried ready-to-eat apricots, quartered
- 200 g (7 oz) dried ready-to-eat prunes, quartered
- 100 g (4 oz) glacé cherries, halved
- 100 g (4 oz) mixed peel
- 75 ml (2 ²/₃ fl oz) brandy, plus extra for maturing
- finely grated zest and juice of 1 orange
- 350 g (12 oz) plain flour
- ¹/₂ teaspoon ground allspice
- ¹/₂ teaspoon ground cinnamon
- ¹/₂ teaspoon freshly grated nutmeg
- 275 g (10 oz) unsalted butter, at room temperature
- 275 g (10 oz) soft dark brown sugar
- 1 tablespoon black treacle
- 5 medium eggs
- 75 g (3 oz) ground almonds

1. Place all the dried and candied fruits in a large bowl and stir in the 75 ml (2 ²/₃ fl oz) brandy and orange zest and juice. Cover and leave in a cool place overnight, stirring a few times. The fruits will absorb the liquid, becoming plump and juicy in the finished cake.

2. Pre-heat the oven to 150°C/300°F/Gas Mark 2.

3. Line the base and sides of a greased 25 cm (10 in) round or 23 cm (9 in) square cake tin with a double layer of baking parchment so it comes about 5 cm (2 in) above the tin. Put a double layer around the outside of the tin, and hold in place with a couple of staples or paper clips. This prevents the cake from overcooking around the outside.

4. Sift together the flour, allspice, cinnamon and nutmeg.

5. In a large bowl or electric mixer, whisk together the butter, sugar and treacle until light and fluffy. Beat in the eggs 1 at a time, adding 1 tablespoon of the flour mixture with each egg. Mix in the almonds and soaked fruits, then carefully fold in the remaining flour mixture.

6. Spoon the mixture into the prepared cake tin, making sure there are no air pockets, and spread evenly across the top. Place the tin in the oven, sitting it on several thicknesses of brown paper or newspaper. After 3 hours, insert a skewer into the centre of the cake. If it comes out clean, the cake is cooked; if not, carry on cooking, testing every 10 minutes. During the cooking time, if the top seems to be darkening too much, cover with a piece of baking parchment.

7. When the cake is cooked, leave in the tin to cool for about an hour and then turn out on to a wire rack. When the cake is completely cold, make several deep holes in it with a skewer and pour over a couple of tablespoons of brandy, which will be absorbed into the cake, giving a richer, more moist finish as it matures. Wrap in a double layer of grease-proof paper or foil and store in a tin. Repeat the moistening process with brandy at regular intervals before Christmas.

TIP

If you like a nutty Christmas cake, add 200 g (7 oz) chopped walnuts, pecans or Brazil nuts (or a mixture of all three) to the cake with the ground almonds.

8

Brandy Butter

Mince pies and Christmas pudding aren't complete without this boozy classic. Brandy butter is four times more popular in the North West of England than in the North East.

Festive Brandy Butter
Makes enough for 12 servings

- 175 g (6 oz) unsalted butter, at room temperature
- 175 g (6 oz) caster sugar
- 4 tablespoons brandy (or extra for a boozy festive touch)
- ½ teaspoon finely grated orange zest

Place all the ingredients in a food processor, or beat with an electric hand whisk until smooth and light in texture and colour. The boozy butter can be used straight away or kept in the fridge; bring it back to room temperature before using.

TIPS
You don't have to use brandy – rum, whisky, Drambuie, Grand Marnier or other flavoured liqueurs are all good alternatives.

For a different texture, soak 50 g (2 oz) finely chopped apricots in the brandy overnight and add to the butter and sugar as above.

2

Crudités with Dips

Is it true that we become more health-conscious as we get older? In our survey, twice as many people aged between 45 and 54 voted crudités their favourite party food compared to the under-25s. They're also the number one party food for vegetarians and for the Welsh.

Rather than using the obvious raw vegetables for crudités (carrot, cucumber, cauliflower, celery and peppers), be adventurous and try some different varieties, or do as the French do and cook them slightly first.

Crudités and Dips   Serves approx. 6–8

- lightly cooked asparagus tips
- flat or runner beans, topped, tailed and cut diagonally into 3–5 cm (1¼–2 in) pieces
- individual leaves of red or white endive/chicory
- individual leaves of Little Gem lettuce
- whole radishes with the stalk attached
- baby turnips, raw or lightly cooked
- scrubbed baby carrots
- raw or lightly cooked baby corn
- thickly sliced fennel

And you don't have to stop at vegetables:

- pitta bread or flour tortillas, cut into wedges, brushed with olive oil and grilled
- breadsticks
- mini cheese biscuits
- thinly sliced French stick, brushed with olive oil and grilled until crispy

WHITE BEAN AND TARRAGON DIP
- 410 g (14½ oz) tin of cannellini or butter beans, drained
- 200 ml (7 fl oz) crème fraîche
- juice of ½ lemon
- ½ teaspoon paprika
- pinch of cayenne pepper
- 1 small clove of garlic, crushed
- 3 tablespoons extra-virgin olive oil
- a small handful of tarragon leaves, chopped
- flaked sea salt and freshly ground black pepper

Place all the ingredients in a food processor and blitz well until really smooth. This tastes best when served at room temperature.

PRAWN AND AVOCADO DIP WITH CHILLI VODKA
- 1 ripe avocado, peeled and stone removed
- 2 tablespoons soured cream
- 150 g (5 oz) cooked prawns, finely chopped
- 1 ripe tomato, quartered, de-seeded and finely diced
- ½ red onion, very finely chopped
- juice of ½ small lemon
- 1 tablespoon chilli-flavoured vodka, or a good splash of Tabasco sauce with a little extra lemon juice
- flaked sea salt and freshly ground black pepper

Mash the avocado with the soured cream until fairly smooth. Mix in all of the remaining ingredients and serve straight away, or chill in the fridge for a few hours.

3

Tapas

Tapa in Spanish means 'lid'; the tradition of tapas with drinks is thought to come from the piece of food that was placed on top of the lid over a drink. The range of tapas is endless, from spicy potatoes (*patatas bravas*) to almonds (*almendras*) and peanuts (*cacahuetes*), prawns (*gambas*) and squid (*calamari*), omelettes (*tortilla*) and smoked spicy sausage (chorizo). Tapas are perfect to serve at an informal party.

Deep-fried Calamari with Garlic and Lemon Mayonnaise
Serves 6–8 as a snack with a drink

- vegetable oil, for deep frying
- 250 g (9 oz) plain flour
- ¹/₂ teaspoon cayenne pepper
- ¹/₂ teaspoon smoked Spanish paprika
- ¹/₂ teaspoon salt
- 500 g (1 lb 2 oz) squid, cut into 5 mm (¹/₄ in) rings
- 2 eggs, beaten

TIP
Many supermarkets and delis sell smoked Spanish paprika. If you can't get hold of any, use the traditional paprika instead

MAYONNAISE
- 200 ml (7 fl oz) mayonnaise
- 1 clove of garlic, crushed
- juice of ¹/₂ lemon

1. For the mayonnaise, mix all the ingredients together and set aside.

2. For the calamari, place enough oil in a wok, large saucepan or deep-fat fryer to come halfway up the pan. Place over a medium heat. If you're using a deep-fat fryer or have a thermometer, heat the oil to 180°C/350°F. If not, to check the oil is at the right temperature, drop a 2–3 cm (³/₄–1 ¹/₄ in) cube of bread into the hot oil. It should become golden and crispy in 1 minute.

3. While the oil is heating, place the flour, cayenne, paprika and salt in a large sandwich bag. Drop in the squid and shake around to coat evenly. This may need to be done in two batches, depending on the size of the bag.

4. Dip the floured squid into the beaten egg and then carefully drop into the hot oil. Fry for 2–3 minutes until golden. Remove from the oil and briefly drain on kitchen paper before serving with the garlic and lemon mayonnaise.

Tortilla Wedges   Serves 6–8 as a snack with a drink

- 6 tablespoons olive oil
- 1 large onion, thinly sliced
- 2 cloves of garlic, crushed
- 4 medium-sized potatoes, thinly sliced
- 5 eggs, lightly beaten
- flaked sea salt and freshly ground black pepper

1. Heat 3 tablespoons of the olive oil in a frying pan and gently fry the onion, garlic and potatoes for about 15 minutes until almost tender. Tip the potato mixture into a large bowl and leave to cool for 5 minutes. Add the beaten eggs and leave to stand for 10 minutes.

2. Place a medium-sized non-stick frying pan, approx. 23–25 cm (9–10 in), over a low heat and add the remaining oil. Season the potato and egg mixture generously with salt and pepper, then pour into the pan. Leave to cook for 15 minutes until almost set.

3. Gently slide the tortilla on to a plate and place another plate on top, flip over and then slide back into the pan, now with the uncooked side down. Continue to cook for a further 5 minutes. Serve warm or at room temperature, cut into wedges.

4   Salad

'Salad' suggests a whole host of different dishes: a basic green salad, but then there's potato salad, pasta salad, rice salad, bean salad, coleslaw, Waldorf, Caesar, Russian, and tomato, mozzarella and avocado, to name but a few.

    This salad can be served either on a large plate or in a bowl for guests to help themselves, or presented in small dishes with chopsticks.

Oriental Chicken Salad
Serves 6 as a main dish, or more if served with other party food

- 4 skinless, boneless chicken breasts
- 4 tablespoons runny honey
- 2 tablespoons rice vinegar
- 2 tablespoons soy sauce
- 1 tablespoon sesame oil
- 1 clove of garlic, crushed
- 2.5 cm (1 in) piece of fresh ginger, peeled and grated
- 2 tablespoons sesame seeds, toasted
- a small bunch of fresh coriander, roughly chopped
- 1 large carrot, cut into fine matchsticks
- 1 bunch of spring onions, shredded
- $\frac{1}{2}$ cucumber, peeled, halved, de-seeded and cut into matchsticks
- $\frac{1}{2}$ Chinese lettuce, finely shredded

1. Cut the chicken into thin strips and mix with the honey, vinegar and soy sauce. Leave to marinate in a non-metallic bowl for about 30 minutes.

2. Heat the sesame oil in a frying pan and cook the chicken over a high heat with any marinade for about 5 minutes until the chicken is cooked through, leaving some cooked marinade in the pan to use as the salad dressing.

3. To serve warm, toss in a large bowl with the remaining ingredients and eat immediaetly. To serve cold, leave the cooked chicken and marinade to cool and then toss with the remaining ingredients.

5   Sausage Rolls

The mainstay of children's parties and a firm favourite with the under-25s, sausage rolls are enjoyed by both men and women alike.

    These are a real step up from traditional sausage rolls – crisp, flaky pastry baked around a tasty sausage filling. The flavours you can add to the filling are endless, so why not double or triple the recipe and make a selection?

Sausage Rolls   Makes 10

- 375 g (13 oz) bought ready-rolled puff pastry
- about 2 tablespoons either chutney of your choice, cranberry sauce, mustard, Branston pickle, apple sauce, pesto, sun-dried tomato paste or red onion jam
- 5 good-quality thick pork sausages
- 1 small egg, beaten

1. Pre-heat the oven to 200°C/400°F/Gas Mark 6.

2. Cut the pastry into 10 rectangles, about 7 x 10 cm (2 $\frac{3}{4}$ x 4 in), and place a small spoonful of your chosen filling into the middle of each one.

3. Cut the sausages in half, making 10 smaller sausages, and then peel away the skins. Lay the sausages on top of the filling on the pastry rectangles. Roll the pastry over the sausage, brushing the join with the beaten egg to seal. Place on a greased baking sheet, sealed-side down, and brush them with the egg to give a nice shiny glaze when cooked.

4. Cook in the oven for 20 minutes until golden and crispy, and eat as soon as they are cool enough or leave to cool completely on a wire rack.

TIP
Try experimenting with some of the flavoured sausages available now, and spread the pastry with a complementary filling.

6

Chicken Drumsticks / Wings

In some ways chicken drumsticks are the ideal party food as you can grab the extending bone in a napkin and gnaw away with ease. Voters in Northern Ireland would heartily agree, as over a quarter put them at the top of their party list. The mistake people often make is to cook them too far in advance so that, by the time of the party, the skin has turned wrinkly and shrivelled and they have lost their appeal.

Satay Chicken with Crunchy Peanut Sauce   Makes 8

- 8 chicken drumsticks or large chicken wings, preferably free-range

MARINADE
- 1 tablespoon soy sauce
- 1 tablespoon runny honey
- 1 teaspoon turmeric
- 1–2 teaspoons ground cumin
- 1–2 teaspoons ground coriander
- 1 clove of garlic, crushed
- 1 cm ($^1/_2$ in) piece of fresh ginger, peeled and finely grated
- squeeze of lime juice
- 1 tablespoon vegetable oil

SAUCE
- 5 tablespoons crunchy peanut butter
- 1 teaspoon Thai red curry paste
- 120 ml (4 fl oz) coconut milk
- 2 teaspoons soft dark brown sugar
- squeeze of lime juice
- a small handful of fresh coriander, roughly chopped (optional)

1. Pierce the chicken drumsticks several times each with a sharp knife and place in a non-metallic bowl.

2. Mix all the marinade ingredients together and stir into the chicken. Leave to marinate for at least 2 hours, or overnight if you can, turning occasionally.

3. Pre-heat the oven to 200°C/400°F/Gas Mark 6.

4. To make the sauce, place all the ingredients, except the coriander, in a small pan and bring to a simmer. Cook for a couple of minutes, stirring occasionally, until thickened. Transfer to a small bowl that's the right size for dipping the chicken drumsticks into, and leave to cool to room temperature. If you're using it, stir in the coriander just before serving.

5. Transfer the chicken pieces into a roasting tray with the marinade. Place in the oven for about 30 minutes, turning occasionally until golden and thoroughly cooked through. To check they're cooked, pierce with a skewer: if the juices run clear, they're done; if the juices are still slightly pink, return to the oven for a further 10 minutes. Serve straight away with the crunchy peanut sauce.

=7   Quiche

When we think of quiche we automatically think of the French classic, quiche Lorraine. The dish actually originated in Germany in the medieval kingdom of Lothringen, later named Lorraine by the French. The word 'quiche' derives from the German *Kuchen*, meaning cake. The ingredients of a classic quiche are just eggs and bacon, with cheese being a much more recent addition. This one has a true Mediterranean taste.

Baby Courgette, Parmesan and Basil Tart   Serves 8

- 250 g (9 oz) bought or home-made puff or shortcrust pastry
- 2 tablespoons olive oil
- 10–12 baby courgettes, halved lengthways
- juice of ¹/₂ lemon
- 2 cloves of garlic, crushed
- 3 eggs
- 300 ml (¹/₂ pint) whipping cream
- 50 g (2 oz) Parmesan cheese, grated
- a handful of basil leaves, torn into pieces, plus extra whole leaves, to serve
- flaked sea salt and freshly ground black pepper
- Parmesan shavings (shave strips of Parmesan from a block with a vegetable peeler) and olive oil, to serve

23 cm (9 in) plain or fluted flan ring, 2.5 cm (1 in) deep

1. Pre-heat the oven to 200°C/400°F/Gas Mark 6.

2. Roll out the pastry thinly to fit the tin, leaving 1 cm (¹/₂ in) of excess pastry hanging over the edge. This allows for shrinking during cooking, and ultimately gives a neater finished result. Place in the fridge for at least 30 minutes.

3. Line the pastry with greaseproof paper and fill with baking beans or rice. Place in the oven for 20 minutes, then remove the greaseproof paper and beans. Return to the oven for a further 5 minutes until the middle of the pastry case is lightly golden. Remove from the oven and leave to cool slightly. With a sharp knife, trim away any excess pastry from the rim, leaving a smooth, even case.

4. Reduce the oven temperature to 180°C/350°F/Gas Mark 4.

5. Heat the oil in a frying pan and fry the baby courgettes for 3–4 minutes, then add the lemon juice and garlic. Cook for about 30 seconds until the lemon juice has evaporated and arrange in the tart case.

6. In a large bowl or jug, beat together the eggs and cream. Add the Parmesan and torn basil leaves and season generously with salt and pepper, then pour over the courgettes in the tart case.

=7   Pizza

Pizza came joint seventh with quiche in our survey to discover the nation's favourite party food. Whereas quiche was the most popular in the North West of England and Scotland, a quarter of the Welsh put pizza top of the list.

There are other pizza recipe suggestions on pages 72–4, but this one uses ciabatta bread as a base rather than the traditional pizza dough, making it more practical to serve as finger food.

Roasted Red Onion, Artichoke and Blue Cheese Ciabatta Pizza

- 2 red onions, each cut into 6 wedges
- few sprigs of thyme
- flaked sea salt and freshly ground black pepper
- olive oil, for drizzling
- 1 part-baked ciabatta
- 1 quantity of Tomato Sauce (see page 72) or 1 medium-sized jar of bought tomato pasta sauce
- 285 g (10$\frac{1}{2}$ oz) jar of marinated artichokes or 400 g (14 oz) tin of artichoke halves, drained and halved
- 120 g (4$\frac{1}{2}$ oz) blue cheese, such as Dolcelatte, Stilton or Gorgonzola, crumbled
- a handful of basil leaves
- a handful of grated Parmesan cheese

1. Pre-heat the oven to 200°C/400°F/Gas Mark 6.

2. Place the onion wedges and thyme in a small roasting tray. Season with salt and pepper and drizzle with olive oil. Place in the oven for 25–30 minutes until softened and beginning to turn golden, turning halfway through.

3. Cut the ciabatta in half lengthways and place on a baking sheet, cut-side down. If the top half of the loaf wobbles around, slice some crust off the base so it sits flat. Spread thickly with the tomato sauce and then sit the roasted onions, artichokes, blue cheese, half the basil leaves and the Parmesan cheese on top. Drizzle over a little oil and add a good twist of black pepper.

4. Bake in the oven for 15 minutes or until the cheese is golden and bubbling and looking and smelling gorgeous. Serve straight away, cut into pieces, with the remaining basil leaves on top.

---

7. Place in the oven and cook for 25 minutes until the egg is just set. Once it's cooked, leave to cool for about 15 minutes before serving. It will taste much better warm rather than piping hot, but remember the flavour will be lost completely if you refrigerate it.

8. Just before serving, scatter with the whole basil leaves and Parmesan shavings and drizzle a little olive oil over the top.

TIP
If you can't get hold of baby courgettes, you can use about 300 g (11 oz) of larger ones – just slice thickly and fry for about 5 minutes longer.

9   Canapés

More women than men chose canapés for a party, especially those in the North West and in the Midlands and East of England.

These recipes, two savoury and two sweet, are ideal for unexpected or last-minute parties. Presentation is important for canapés, so lay them uniformly on large, flat plates and space them out evenly to give a sophisticated look and to create the impression that you've spent hours preparing them.

Cucumber and Tuna Bites
Makes 12–15

- 200 g (7 oz) tin of tuna, drained and flaked
- 1–2 tablespoons olive oil
- a small handful of chopped fresh parsley
- good squeeze of lemon juice
- ½ small red onion, finely chopped
- flaked sea salt and freshly ground black pepper
- olives, capers or anchovies, finely chopped (optional)
- 1 cucumber

1. Mix the tuna with the olive oil, parsley, lemon juice and red onion and season with salt and pepper. You can also add a few finely chopped olives, capers or anchovies if you like.

2. Cut the cucumber into 5 mm–1 cm (¼–½ in) thick slices (peeled if you prefer) and sit small spoonfuls of the tuna mixture on top of each one. Arrange neatly on a large serving plate.

Peach, Stilton and Parma Ham Wraps
Make as many as you like

- fresh peaches (if you don't have fresh, use tinned)
- Stilton cheese
- Parma ham (or any good dry-cured ham such as Black Forest, Serrano or prosciutto)
- freshly ground black pepper
- olive oil for drizzling

1. Cut the peaches into fairly thick wedges, then slice the Stilton to approximately the same size. Place a peach wedge and piece of Stilton together and wrap in half a strip of Parma ham. Continue in this way until you have used all the peaches, Stilton and ham.

2. Season with pepper and drizzle over some olive oil. Arrange neatly on a large serving plate.

Jamaican Ginger Cubes
Makes approx. 36

- 1 bought Jamaican
  ginger cake
- couple of balls of stem
  ginger in syrup

Cut the Jamaican ginger cake into 2 cm (³/₄ in) squares and line up neatly on a large, flat plate. Finely chop the stem ginger and add some to the top of each piece. Spoon over a little of the ginger syrup and serve.

Juicy Fruits with Lemon Cream
Make as many as you like

- lemon curd
- crème fraîche or natural yoghurt
- ripe strawberries, cherries, grapes; cubes of melon, pineapple, kiwi fruit, peaches, nectarines, mango or papaya

Mix together one third lemon curd to two thirds crème fraîche or natural yoghurt. Transfer to a small dish and dip fresh and deliciously ripe strawberries, cherries, grapes, and cubes of melon, pineapple, kiwi fruit, peaches, nectarines, mango or papaya into the cream.

TIP
If the strawberries seem shallow in taste, add a twist of black pepper, which will bring out a fuller flavour.

10

Sausage on a Stick

A sausage on a stick can be the best or the worst food at a party. If the sausages are cold and wrinkled and served sticking out of a 'hedgehog', they're only going to appeal to children. But if they're freshly cooked, hot and sticky, your guests won't be able to resist.

Honey, Mustard and Sesame-glazed Sausages   Makes 20

- 20 cocktail sausages
- 2 tablespoons runny honey
- $\frac{1}{2}$ teaspoon English mustard
- $1\frac{1}{2}$ tablespoons sesame seeds

1. Pre-heat the oven to 180°C/350°F/Gas Mark 4.

2. Sit the sausages on a baking tray in a single layer. Place in the oven and cook for about 15 minutes, turning occasionally, until golden and cooked through.

3. In a medium-sized bowl, mix together the honey, mustard and sesame seeds. Add the cooked sausages and stir around so they all get a good sticky coating. Return to the baking tray with any remaining flavoured honey mixture spooned over and put back in the oven for 8 minutes until bubbling, sticky and irresistible.

4. Leave to cool slightly and serve hot or warm – and of course they wouldn't be complete without the cocktail sticks to pick them up. You can also try the following glazes with the sausages (cook in the same way):

SPICY TOMATO

- $1\frac{1}{2}$ tablespoons tomato ketchup
- $\frac{1}{2}$ teaspoon chilli powder
- 1 teaspoon brown sugar

MAPLE AND ROSEMARY

- 1 tablespoon maple syrup
- 2 teaspoons finely chopped fresh rosemary

10:
Nation's Favourite
Festive Food

There is just one day of the year when most people across the country eat an identical meal. The day is 25 December and the traditional Christmas dinner has been voted the nation's number one food for festivities. An astonishing 65 per cent of those who voted in our survey put roast turkey at the top of the festive food list, but in Northern Ireland the figure was even higher – 84 per cent said they enjoyed it more than any other food for festive occasions.

Britain has such a diverse mix of cultures that there are different festive occasions almost every month of the year. After seeing in the New Year in January, festivities in February include Shrove Tuesday, Chinese New Year and Eid-ul-Adha for Muslims. Mothering Sunday in March was traditionally known as Simnel Sunday, when Christians visited a 'mother church' and took gifts, including simnel cake, to their mothers. We now associate the cake, with its twelve marzipan balls representing the Apostles, with Easter. Matzah or unleavened bread is eaten for Jewish Passover in March or April, and Christians mark Good Friday with hot cross buns, and give chocolate eggs on Easter Sunday to represent new life. In July or August Hindus and Sikhs hold a festival to honour the relationship between brothers and sisters, when Indian sweets are exchanged between siblings. The end of summer is marked by displays of food in churches around the country to celebrate

harvest festival, and autumn is hailed with fireworks both on Guy Fawkes night and Diwali, a Hindu and Sikh festival of lights, in November. December comes around all too quickly, with the eight-day festival Hanukkah taking priority for the Jewish community, and the Christmas holiday period when everyone can enjoy a well-earned rest.

All these events are firmly linked with the family and should be a time for everyone to come together and share some memorable occasions and delicious food. Indian cookery writer Madhur Jaffrey loves to spend Christmas with her family: 'As far as I'm concerned, it's a time to bring the family together and make them all feel a part of something unchanging and that they belong with each other. You are together at the table but you're also together in the kitchen, and then you're together cleaning up, so the whole process is done with great solidarity. In a very changing, frightening world, especially for little children, I think it gives them a great anchor.'

Gary Rhodes remembers what Christmas was like for him as a child: 'You used to get up very early and you were convinced you were the first up. And then you'd smell something roasting and you'd think, "What's going on? It's six o'clock in the morning!" But somehow the bird was already in the oven, the day had arrived. When I think about it now it was that turkey smell that used to wake us up. Christmas was all about sitting at the table, but as a child you couldn't really get excited about the lunch. You wanted the party spirit, you wanted the cracker and the little hat, but as far as the food was concerned, well, I never did like sprouts.'

Although we included a long list of festive foods to vote for in our survey, it was only the food traditionally served at Christmas and Easter that made it into the top ten. You may like to make some of the following recipes as presents for friends and family. What could be nicer than a home-made Christmas pud or a hand-made Easter egg personally decorated by someone you love?

1 Roast Turkey and All the Trimmings

Turkeys were introduced to this country from the Americas as early as the sixteenth century and quickly became the popular meat for a Christmas feast. It's a lot of work to prepare a meal of this stature, but if you're well organized and have family and friends to help, it's a feast that will give a huge amount of pleasure to everyone.

Succulent Roast Turkey   Serves 6–8

TURKEY
- 4.5–5.5 kg (10–12 lb) oven-ready turkey, preferably free-range
- flaked sea salt and freshly ground black pepper
- 2 onions, halved
- 1 bulb of garlic, halved to see the cloves in cross section
- 3–4 fresh bay leaves
- 120 g (4 1/2 oz) butter, at room temperature
- grated zest of 1/2 lemon
- handful of sage leaves, chopped

SHERRY GRAVY
- 2 tablespoons flour
- 600 ml (1 pint) hot turkey or chicken stock
- good splash of dry sherry
- 2–3 tablespoons double cream

1. You can prepare the turkey on Christmas Eve. Remove the giblets; you can use them to make your own stock. Wipe the turkey inside and out with kitchen paper. Season inside with salt and pepper, then put in the onions, garlic and bay leaves.

2. Mix together the butter with 2 teaspoons each of salt and pepper, the lemon zest and chopped sage. Spread all over the turkey and cover the breast meat with a double piece of greaseproof paper to stop it drying out during cooking. The turkey can be put in the fridge until the morning.

3. Remove the turkey from the fridge as early as possible on Christmas Day, to allow it to reach room temperature before cooking. Pre-heat the oven to 220°C/425°F/Gas Mark 7.

4. To work out the cooking times, allow 30 minutes on the high heat (220°C/425°F/Gas Mark 7), then reduce the temperature (see below) and cook for 30 minutes per 1 kg (2 1/4 lb), so a 4.5 kg (10 lb) turkey will take about 3 hours and a 5.5 kg (12 lb) turkey will take about 3 hours 30 minutes.

5. Place the turkey on a rack or trivet in a large roasting tray. Pour a cup of hot water into the bottom of the tray and cover the whole thing with a double piece of foil. Doing this will add moisture to the turkey during the long roasting time. Place the bird in the oven and, after 30 minutes, reduce the temperature to 200°C/400°F/Gas Mark 6. Roast for a further hour, then remove the foil and greaseproof paper. Now leave the turkey to continue roasting without opening the oven door again until the cooking time is up and the skin is wonderfully crisp and golden. To check the turkey is thoroughly cooked through, insert a skewer where the thigh joins the breast. If the juices run clear, it's cooked; if not, continue to roast for a further 15 minutes, then test again.

6. Transfer the turkey to a large plate or board, ready for carving. Cover loosely with foil and keep in a warm place to rest for up to 45 minutes, giving you time to cook any vegetables and trimmings.

7. To make the gravy, pour away any excess fat from the tray and place the tray over a high heat. Stir in the flour, scraping up any sticky bits from the bottom of the tray. Gradually pour in the stock and sherry and simmer until slightly thickened. To finish, stir in the double cream, add salt and pepper if needed and strain through a sieve for a smooth gravy.

(CONTINUED OVERLEAF)